Raymond E. Brown, S.S.

A Coming Christ in Advent

Essays on the Gospel Narratives
Preparing for the Birth of Jesus
Matthew 1 and Luke 1

The Liturgical Press
Collegeville, Minnesota

The essays reprinted here were originally published (under the usual rule of ecclesiastical approbation) as follows:
Most of the material in Chapter 1 in *Catholic Update* (November 1986) and *St. Anthony's Messenger* 94 (November 1986) 482–490.
Chapter 2 in *Worship* 60 (November 1986) 482–490.
Chapter 3 in *Worship* 61 (November 1987) 482–492.
Chapters 4 and 5 in *Worship* (November 1988) 482–496.
Chapter 6 in *Worship* (May 1988) 249–259.

Cover design by Mary Jo Pauly

6   7   8   9

Library of Congress Cataloging in Publication Data

Brown, Raymond Edward.
    A coming Christ in Advent : essays on the Gospel narratives preparing for the Birth of Jesus : Matthew I and Luke I / Raymond E. Brown.
        p.   cm.
    ISBN 0-8146-1587-2 (pbk.) .
    1. Bible. N.T. Matthew I—Criticism, interpretation, etc.
2. Bible. N.T. Luke I—Criticism, interpretation, etc. 3. Jesus Christ—Nativity.   I. Title.
BS2575.2.B77   1988
226'.206—dc19   88-10168
                                                              CIP

Contents

Foreword   5

Chapter 1 The Origin and Purpose of the
           Infancy Narratives   7

Chapter 2 The Genealogy of Jesus Christ
           (Matthew 1:1-17)   16

Chapter 3 The Annunciation to Joseph
           (Matthew 1:18-25)   27

Chapter 4 The Annunciation to Zechariah and
           the Birth of the Baptist (Luke 1:5-25,
           57-66, 80)   40

Chapter 5 The Benedictus (Luke 1:67-79)   49

Chapter 6 The Annunciation to Mary, the
           Visitation, and the Magnificat
           (Luke 1:26-56)   60

Foreword

In previous Liturgical Press volumes I have written essays on the Passion Narratives for the Lenten season (*A Crucified Christ in Holy Week*) and on the second part of the Infancy Narratives for the Christmas season (*An Adult Christ at Christmas*). The latter discussed in a popular manner the *aftermath* of Jesus' birth as described in chapter 2 of Matthew's Gospel (the magi and the star) and in chapter 2 of Luke (the shepherds, the manger, the presentation of Jesus in the Temple, and the finding of the boy Jesus in the Temple). I wish here to complete my reflections on the Infancy Narratives by discussing in a similar way chapter 1 of Matthew and chapter 1 of Luke—what happened by way of *preparation* for the birth of Jesus. Logically the Advent season is the time when the church treats this material in her liturgy, preparing the way for the coming of Christ at Christmas.

This liturgical preparation relives in a microcosmic way the long historical preparation for the coming of Christ in the history of Israel (seen through the eyes of Christian faith). It is no accident that in the first chapter of the Gospel both Matthew (explicitly) and Luke (implicitly) turn to that history and begin their narrative with the story of Abraham and Sarah conceiving Isaac. For the evangelists that was already the beginning of the story of Jesus Christ. As narrated in the Law and the Prophets, the God who acted in Israel, often with surprising graciousness in the lives of the patriarchs, the judges, and the kings, is the same God who is acting again with surprising graciousness in the lives of Joseph and Mary as He reveals what He is going to accomplish. Thus the Advent liturgy in retelling the first chapter of Matthew and the first chapter of Luke is also retelling the story of Israel which lies beneath it. One might think of a double exposure where the older picture is seen through the more visible picture that emerges on top.

The Messiah did not come without the preparatory period of Israel's history or without the preparatory responses of fidelity by Joseph and Mary. The liturgy offers a third time of preparation that affects our lives, for Christ will not come in his fullness to us unless we too are prepared. This small book attempts to use Matthew 1 and Luke 1 as they are read in the last days of Advent to inform that preparation, so that our answer to God's invitation may be as affirmative as those of our ancestors in Israel and in the New Testament period.

I dedicate this book in friendship and gratitude to Professor John Kselman, S.S., now teaching at Weston School of Theology in Cambridge, Massachusetts. We first met some thirty-five years ago, and later it was my privilege to teach him during his theological seminary years. For two decades he has rendered me the inestimable service of reading in typescript everything I write ("Greater love no man hath"), correcting errors (typographical and otherwise), and suggesting improvements of phraseology and points I missed. Thus not only am I in his debt, but so too are those who graciously read my books. This public acknowledgment given to such a generous scholar is small return indeed.

Union Theological Seminary, N.Y.C. 10027
Feast of the Epiphany, 6 January 1988

Foreword

6

Chapter 1

The Origin and Purpose of the Infancy Narratives

The heart of this book will be a discussion of the biblical text of Matthew 1 and Luke 1 as an Advent preparation for the coming of Christ. But readers unfamiliar with the peculiar character of the Infancy Narratives may well find useful a general introduction explaining why and how these stories were written. This chapter will attempt to do that simply and concisely.

WHY ARE THERE GOSPEL STORIES OF JESUS' INFANCY? Surprisingly in the whole New Testament only two authors pay attention to Jesus' birth and childhood—only Matthew and Luke give us "Infancy Narratives."

Most scholars think that Mark was the first Gospel to be written, but it begins with the baptism of Jesus by John. It tells us nothing of Jesus' earlier family existence, never even mentioning Joseph, his legal father. In this approach Mark is far from alone in early Christianity, for the other twenty-four books of the New Testament (outside Matthew and Luke) are like Mark in failing to show interest in Jesus' family origins before he began the ministry. Even John who starts his Gospel, not with the baptism but with the divine Word before creation, ignores the family circumstances in which the Word became flesh.

What then caused Matthew and Luke to begin with a story of Jesus' conception and birth? One probable factor was curiosity about the origins of this Jesus who was hailed as God's Son. Were his beginnings marked with the divine power that characterized his ministry? Mere curiosity, however, would not explain the judgment that Jesus' infancy should be made

Infancy Narratives: Origin and Purpose

part of a written Gospel. Neither Matthew nor Luke was composing simply a life of Jesus; and for information about his birth to be part of their "good news" it had to have religious value—a value that is the key to understanding the Infancy Narratives. Indeed, as we shall see, despite the fact that the two evangelists fashioned very different birth stories, they agreed remarkably in a common religious message about the conception of Jesus.

If it comes as a shock to many Christians to find that Matthew and Luke are our only sources for knowledge about Jesus' infancy, it may be an even greater shock to realize that the two Gospels differ so much. Our Christmas crib or creche scenes combine them; but if you pick up the New Testament without previous assumptions and read separately Matthew 1–2 and Luke 1–2, the enormous difference is obvious.

Matthew gives a picture wherein Mary and Joseph live at Bethlehem and have a house there. The coming of the magi, guided by the star, causes Herod to slay children at Bethlehem and the Holy Family to flee to Egypt. The fact that Herod's son Archelaus rules in Judea after him makes Joseph afraid to return to Bethlehem, and so he takes the child and his mother to Galilee to the town of Nazareth—obviously for the first time.

Luke, on the other hand, tells us that Mary and Joseph lived at Nazareth and went to Bethlehem only temporarily because they had to register there during a Roman census. The statement that Mary gave birth to her child and laid him in a manger because there was no place for them in "the inn" implies that they had no house of their own in Bethlehem. And Luke's account of the peaceful return of the Holy Family from Bethlehem through Jerusalem to Nazareth leaves no room for the coming of the magi or a struggle with Herod.

Some scholars have tried very hard to reconcile the differ-

Infancy Narratives: Origin and Purpose

ences between Matthew and Luke but with little convincing success. A greater fidelity to Scripture as we have received it would recognize that the Holy Spirit was content to give us two different accounts and that the way to interpret them faithfully is to treat them separately. Sometimes the drive to harmonize them arises from the false idea that, since Scripture is inspired, each infancy account must be completely historical. For some fifty years since Pope Pius XII, the Catholic Church has taught firmly and clearly that the Bible is a library handed down to us by Israel and the early church. In that collection of inspired books there are many different types of literature, including poetry, drama, history, and fiction. Indeed, between history and fiction there is a whole range of possibilities covering imaginative retellings that have a core of fact.

The birth stories differ from the New Testament accounts of Jesus' ministry and death where *known eyewitnesses,* the apostles, are presented as the sources of the traditional preaching embodied in the Gospels and the Book of Acts. Some may object that Matthew and Luke surely got their information about Jesus' birth from his parents. Yet that is never claimed in the New Testament, nor in the earliest church writings; and the great difference between the two Gospels' birth stories causes difficulty for that solution. Nor does the rest of the New Testament offer any confirming echo of what is told us in the Infancy Narratives. Hard to reconcile are a great commotion at Jesus' birth and a public revelation as to who he was with the fact that, later when he comes to be baptized, he is an unknown and no one at Nazareth expects him to be a religious figure. We must content ourselves that there is no way to know precisely how historical the Infancy Narratives are, or to know where Matthew and Luke got them. Thus we avoid both a naive fundamentalism that would take every word of these accounts as literal history and a destructive skepticism that would reduce

Infancy Narratives: Origin and Purpose

them to sheer mythology. (As will be seen below, the items on which the two accounts agree militate against the purely fictional approach and must be taken seriously.)

Does this limitation of our knowledge take away value from them? Not at all. Too much worry about historicity and sources of information distracts from the inspired meaning of the biblical text, which is centered on what the two evangelists were trying to teach us—the religious message on which they both agree. There are two major points in that message: first, the identity of Jesus; second, his role as the dramatic embodiment of the whole of Israel's history.

THE IDENTITY OF JESUS

Matthew and Luke agree that Jesus' descent is to be traced genealogically through Joseph who was of the house of David. According to Jewish law, Joseph's acknowledgment of Jesus would make him the legal father of the child (a status not dependent on physical fatherhood), and so Jesus was truly a Son of David. Matthew and Luke agree that Mary conceived Jesus not through sexual relations with Joseph but by the creative power of the Holy Spirit. Thus Jesus was truly the Son of God. This dual identity, Son of David and Son of God, was a very important component in the New Testament conception of gospel or "good news."

When Paul was writing to the Roman Christians about the year A.D. 58 and assuring this community whom he had not converted that he preached the same gospel that they knew, he phrased his description of Jesus thus: "Born of the seed of David according to the flesh; designated Son of God in power according to the Holy Spirit as of resurrection from the dead" (Rom 1:3-4). This is the same twofold identity found in the two Infancy Narratives, but in Paul (who wrote earlier than Matthew and Luke) sonship through the Holy Spirit is attached to the resurrection. Elsewhere an affirmation of both divine and Davidic sonship is attached to the

Infancy Narratives: Origin and Purpose

baptism of Jesus. For instance, in Luke's account of the baptism (3:21ff.), God declares to Jesus, "You are my beloved Son" while the Holy Spirit descends on Jesus; and Luke then gives a genealogy tracing Jesus' descent from David and the patriarchs. In other words, as Christians reflected on Jesus' life, the great "moments" of that life (the resurrection, the baptism, and eventually the conception) were used to clarify who he was: the Messiah or anointed King of the house of David and the unique Son of God through the Holy Spirit. When and because birth stories became the vehicle of that message, they could appropriately be included in the written Gospels.

Many other essential aspects of the gospel message about the identity of Jesus are taught us by the Infancy Narratives. In both Matthew and Luke this identity is proclaimed by an angel as God's messenger. Similarly, Paul insists that he did not receive his gospel from human sources, but God "was pleased to reveal His Son" (Gal 1:12, 16). And in Matthew 16:16-17, Peter's confession of Jesus as Messiah, the Son of God, is hailed by Jesus as "not revealed by flesh and blood but by my Father in heaven." In the baptismal accounts of Mark, Matthew, and Luke, God's voice speaks from heaven about His Son. Thus there was a fundamental understanding that the identity of Jesus was a divine revelation, not a human deduction.

Another common feature in the two Gospels is the insistence that the identity of Jesus was quickly shared with others. In Matthew the revelation given to Joseph is in God's plan made known to the Gentile magi. In Luke the revelation given to Mary is in God's plan made known to the Jewish shepherds. Although the cast of characters differs sharply, the evangelists are each in his own way teaching us that Christ's identity is never received to be kept a private possession. And in God's providence, there are others eager to receive it, even if those others are not the ones we might have expected.

Infancy Narratives: Origin and Purpose

There is a negative side also to the agreement of the two evangelists: a warning that not all will accept the gospel, especially some who should have been eager. If the magi come without hesitation to worship Jesus, guided by the star and, even more specifically, by the prophetic words of Scripture (Matt 2:2-6), the king and the chief priests and the scribes who possess the Jewish heritage and can read the Scriptures easily are quite hostile to Jesus. If Luke describes the rejoicing of the shepherds and of Simeon and Anna over the birth of "a Savior who is Christ the Lord" (2:11), there is nevertheless a solemn warning that this child is set for the fall as well as the rise of many in Israel, a sign to be contradicted who will cause the hostile thoughts of many to be revealed (2:34-35). In other words, the Christmas crib lies under the shadow of the cross; the gospel is always a factor that produces judgment; and the joy of the "good news" has also an element of sadness because not all will believe.

In a very real way, then, the Infancy Narratives of Matthew and Luke are whole gospels. They contain the basic revelation of the full identity of Jesus and the way in which this revelation was quickly shared with others, evangelizing some, but causing rejection and hatred among others.

THE EMBODIMENT OF ISRAEL'S HISTORY

There is a second religious message on which Matthew and Luke agree that goes beyond the identity of Jesus, and this second message may be even more necessary to proclaim today since so few Christians appreciate it. When Matthew and Luke wrote, the Scriptures of the Christian community consisted of what would later be called the Old Testament—there was not yet a New Testament. Those Scriptures were known to Jews as "the Law, the Prophets and the other books." Both Matthew and Luke used their first two chapters, the Infancy Narratives, as a transition from these Jewish Scriptures to the story of Jesus' ministry. The evangelists made a sum-

Infancy Narratives: Origin and Purpose

mary of Old Testament stories and motifs because they felt it impossible to appreciate Jesus without such preparation.

This Old Testament context is often very foreign to Christians today, especially to Catholic audiences; and, alas, they hear little preaching about it. Working with the Infancy Narratives, priests and catechists might well use the Advent period to proclaim the Jewish Scriptures as a setting with which the church begins her liturgical year. (Concentration on the Bible is often far more effective when people see how it fits in with the church's liturgy in which they worship God.) The chapters that follow in this book will explain in detail how Matthew and Luke incorporate Old Testament background in their Infancy Narratives, but let me give a brief overview here.

Matthew begins "the story of the origin of Jesus Christ" (1:1) with Abraham begetting Isaac. His genealogical list of names resumes in capsule form the story of the patriarchs and the rise and fall of the monarchy from David to the Babylonian Exile. We learn a lesson from the names that separate Zerubbabel from Joseph at the end of the list: these were people too insignificant to be mentioned in Israel's history, but they were significant to God as He prepared for the Messiah. Then in a double-exposure technique Matthew's story of the conception and birth of Jesus reenacts the story of Israel's deliverance from Egypt. Joseph the father of Jesus is deliberately reminiscent of the Old Testament Joseph, as he receives revelation in dreams and goes to Egypt, thus saving the family. The wicked king Herod is a carbon copy of the wicked Pharaoh who killed the Hebrew male children, only to have God protect the life of the one who would save his people (Moses=Jesus). In the story of Moses, the Magus Balaam came from the East and saw the star of the Davidic king rise from Israel (Nm 22–24); so too after Jesus' birth magi come from the East, having seen the star of the King of the Jews. Matthew fortifies these reminiscences from the saga

Infancy Narratives: Origin and Purpose

of Moses recounted in Old Testament Books of the Law (Pentateuch) with five pertinent quotations from the Prophets, so that the fulfillment of the Law and the Prophets may be seen as an introduction to what God will do through Jesus when the Gospel proper begins with the baptism at the Jordan.

Luke uses a similar double exposure to tell the story of Israel and of Jesus' infancy at the same time, but his technique is more subtle than Matthew's. Zechariah and Elizabeth, the parents of John the Baptist, are portrayed as similar to Abraham and Sarah in Genesis, the first Book of the Law. The messenger of revelation is Gabriel, the angel of the endtime who appears in Daniel, the last book of the Hebrew Scriptures to be composed—thus Luke covers the range of the Old Testament. The annunciations of the conception of the Baptist and of Jesus echo Old Testament birth annunciations. The four canticles that enhance the Lucan Infancy Narrative (Magnificat, Benedictus, Gloria in Excelsis, Nunc Dimittis) are a mosaic of Old Testament recollections, with almost every line parallel to a verse from the Prophets and the Psalms. Mary's presentation of Jesus in the Temple echoes Hannah's presentation of Samuel at the shrine in 1 Samuel 1:24-28. In the story of Jesus' youth from his circumcision to his rearing at Nazareth a constant refrain is that everything was done according to the Law of the Lord. For Luke the infancy chapters bridge the Jewish Scriptures and the Gospel of Jesus—a bridge on which Old Testament characters like Zechariah, Elizabeth, Simeon, and Anna meet with Gospel figures like the Baptist, Mary, and Jesus.

***

As we turn now to a consideration of scenes from chapter 1 of Matthew and chapter 1 of Luke, we should keep in mind the twofold religious message just described. The one whose coming we anticipate in Advent is Son of David and Son of God. As Son of David he is heir to all the history of Israel so allusively described beneath the surface of the birth stories.

Infancy Narratives: Origin and Purpose

As Son of God he embodies that divine grace which always goes beyond expectation. The Old Testament past illustrates God's gracious mercy even to the unworthy: He has always lifted up the lowly; He has always heard the prayers of the faithful and obedient. Now His Son will share revelation and grace even more widely for the glory of Israel and a light to the Gentiles.

Infancy Narratives: Origin and Purpose

Chapter 2

The Genealogy of Jesus Christ (Matthew 1:1-17)

¹The story of the origin of Jesus Christ, son of David, son of Abraham:

²Abraham was the father of Isaac;
Isaac was the father of Jacob;
Jacob was the father of Judah and his brothers;
³Judah was the father of Perez and Zerah by *Tamar*;
Perez was the father of Hezron;
Hezron was the father of Aram;
⁴Aram was the father of Amminadab;
Amminadab was the father of Nahshon;
Nahshon was the father of Salmon;
⁵Salmon was the father of Boaz by *Rahab*;
Boaz was the father of Obed by *Ruth*;
Obed was the father of Jesse;
⁶Jesse was the father of David the king.

David was the father of Solomon by *Uriah's wife*;
⁷Solomon was the father of Rehoboam;
Rehoboam was the father of Abijah;
Abijah was the father of Asaph;
⁸Asaph was the father of Jehoshaphat;
Jehoshaphat was the father of Joram;
Joram was the father of Uzziah;
⁹Uzziah was the father of Jotham;
Jotham was the father of Ahaz;
Ahaz was the father of Hezekiah;
¹⁰Hezekiah was the father of Manasseh;
Manasseh was the father of Amos;
Amos was the father of Josiah;
¹¹Josiah was the father of Jechoniah and his brothers
at the time of the Babylonian Exile.

Genealogy of Jesus

¹²After the Babylonian Exile,
Jechoniah was the father of Shealtiel;
Shealtiel was the father of Zerubbabel;
¹³Zerubbabel was the father of Abiud;
Abiud was the father of Eliakim;
Eliakim was the father of Azor;
¹⁴Azor was the father of Zadok;
Zadok was the father of Achim;
Achim was the father of Eliud;
¹⁵Eliud was the father of Eleazar;
Eleazar was the father of Matthan;
Matthan was the father of Jacob;
¹⁶Jacob was the father of Joseph, the husband of *Mary*;
of her was begotten Jesus, called the Christ.

¹⁷Thus the total generations from Abraham to David were fourteen generations; and from David to the Babylonian Exile fourteen more generations; and finally from the Babylonian Exile to the Christ fourteen more generations.

***

This genealogy that opens Matthew's Gospel has one principal occurrence in liturgy, namely, on the Advent weekday December 17 which begins the pre-Christmas octave of infancy gospel readings.[1] It was read more frequently in the pre-Vatican II liturgy, but often with disastrous results as the priest-celebrant stumbled over names and sometimes skipped large sections, under the pretense that the reading was a boring and meaningless exercise. To the contrary I have been conducting a somewhat solitary campaign to make this Matthean genealogy a major Advent topic, even to the extent that, if I am invited to give a special pre-Christmas sermon, especially on an Advent Sunday, I go out of my way to make Matthew 1:1-17 the subject of the homily. The stunned

[1]It is also assigned to the afternoon Mass on December 24—a Mass that seems not to be frequently celebrated in the U.S.A.

Genealogy of Jesus

look on the faces of the parish audience when I launch into the solemn list of begettings is proof that one of the prerequisites for effective preaching has been accomplished— attention has been caught, even if the initial impression may be that the selection of the Gospel pericope is slightly daft.

As a preliminary to comment on the genealogy, let me make a series of remarks to highlight its importance. If a Christian today were asked to tell someone who knows nothing about Christianity the basic story of Jesus Christ, where would he or she be likely to begin? I am willing to wager that not one in ten thousand would begin where the author of the Gospel that the church puts first begins—where the first line of the first page of the New Testament begins—with the majestic assurance: This is "the story of the beginning/the origin/the genesis of Jesus Christ." Indeed, we might approximate: "the story of the advent of Jesus Christ."[2] For Matthew the origin of Jesus Christ starts with Abraham begetting Isaac! In other words the story of the Hebrew patriarchs, of the kings of Judah, and of other Israelites is the opening stage of the story of Jesus Christ. That such an Old Testament component to the Jesus story would not occur to most Christians today is a sad commentary on how far we have moved from our ancestors' understanding of the good news. Matthew's list of people who are an integral part of the origin of Jesus Christ contains some of the most significant names in the biblical account of God's dealing with His people Israel, and I for one wish strongly that at least once a year their names were allowed to resound in the Christian church on a Sunday when all the worshiping New Testament people of God were there to hear.

The Matthean sense of the genesis or origin or advent of Jesus Christ, however, goes beyond recalling the Old Testa-

[2]The Greek is literally: "The book of the genesis of Jesus Christ"; that expression probably plays on the literal meaning plus the Septuagintal rendering of the Hebrew term for "genealogical record."

Genealogy of Jesus

ment; and that is why I would insist it must be *preached*. I am not at all the first to claim this. In thinking about the initiators of the Protestant Reformation most Roman Catholics would recall Martin Luther and John Calvin; but there was a third famous Reformer, perhaps the most radical, Ulrich Zwingli, who was based in Switzerland. While he was still a functioning Catholic priest, he became pastor of the Cathedral of Zurich. Already imbued with the growing stress on the supreme importance of Scripture, he conceived the idea of preaching on the whole New Testament—yes, from the first verse of Matthew to the last verse of Revelation—an idea that in a sense found ultimate acceptance in the Catholic Church after Vatican II with the three-year lectionary of readings that cover most of the New Testament and invite even daily homilies. Accordingly, in January 1519 Zwingli began his project by preaching on the Matthean genealogy, a homiletic challenge that would have caused most preachers then and there to retreat in despair. But Zwingli maintained that if one understood it correctly, this genealogy contained the essential theology of the Reformation. I would be even bolder: it contains the essential theology of the Old and the New Testaments that the whole Church, Orthodox, Roman Catholic, and Protestant, should proclaim. Let me illustrate this by comments on the three sections of the genealogy.

THE PATRIARCHS

"The story of the origin of Jesus Christ" begins with the patriarchal period when Abraham begets Isaac. With even a catechism knowledge of Bible stories the hearer might remember with a little puzzlement that Abraham had two sons of whom Ishmael was the older and wonder why the story of the origin of Jesus Christ does not involve the begetting of Ishmael who with his mother Hagar was the more abused figure. (Indeed their story constitutes one of those

Genealogy of Jesus

tales of terror of which Phyllis Trible writes.[3]) The puzzlement should increase when "the story of the origin of Jesus Christ" goes on with Isaac begetting Jacob. Here too there was another, older brother Esau—a bit of a clod, it is true, but in his rustic way more honest than the calculating, deceptive Jacob who, *salva reverentia* to Augustine, was more a liar than a mystery when he stole the birthright. (It is to the credit of Old Testament Israel that it recognized that its own seizure of the land of Canaan had elements of usurpation from other peoples who had a prior claim, a usurpation hinted at by what it attributed to its eponymous ancestor Jacob/Israel.)

The puzzling "story of the origin of Jesus Christ" goes on with Jacob begetting Judah and his brothers. Why is Judah singled out, and why ultimately is the Messiah from his tribe? Was not Joseph clearly the best of the brothers? Favored by God with visionary dreams that aroused the hatred of the others, Joseph forgave their selling him into captivity in Egypt and saved them when they would have perished from starvation in the famine. Surely he is the embodiment of Jesus' story, not Judah who sold his brother and sought out prostitutes.

Matthew's choice of Isaac over Ishmael, of Jacob over Esau, of Judah over Joseph is faithful to the Old Testament insight that God frequently does not choose the best or the noble or the saintly. In other words, Matthew is faithful to an insight about a God who is not controlled by human merit but manifests His own unpredictable graciousness. No wonder Zwingli saw here the theology of the Reformation (which in this case is simply the theology of both Testaments), a theology of salvation by grace. Truly this theology, at work in the choices among the patriarchs, is "the beginning story of Jesus Christ," since he will preach salvation to tax collectors

[3]*Texts of Terror* (Philadelphia: Fortress, 1984) 8–35.

Genealogy of Jesus

and sinners, proclaim that they need a physician and not those who are already religious, and who will ultimately die for us "while we were still sinners" (Rom 5:8). Matthew's genealogy is telling us that the story of Jesus Christ contains as many sinners as saints and is written with the crooked lines of liars and betrayers and the immoral, and not only with straight lines.

THE KINGS

But perhaps one may object that in concentrating on the patriarchal beginnings of the story, I am giving undue emphasis to the rude and the primitive. Does not the first section of Matthew's genealogy build up from Abraham to the high point of "David the king"? And does not the second section of the genealogy consist of the gloriously reigning Judean kings of the house of David? The answer to both those questions invokes the basic biblical issue of God's values versus human appearances—"My thoughts are not your thoughts," says the Lord (Is 55:8). Seemingly the first part of the genealogy does build up from an Abraham who had no land but received a promise to a David who rules as king in possession of this promised land. But the second part of the genealogy calls into question whether that really was a progressive buildup, for it shows that the monarchy went downhill from David the king to "the deportation to Babylon." In other words, it goes from possessing the land to losing it. As for gloriously reigning monarchs of the house of David, of the fourteen Judean kings that Matthew lists between David and the deportation only two (Hezekiah and Josiah) could be considered as faithful to God's standards in the law code of Deuteronomy, which were applied to the monarchs by the author of the Books of Kings. The rest were an odd assortment of idolaters, murderers, incompetents, power-seekers, and harem-wastrels.

David himself was a stunning combination of saint and sin-

Genealogy of Jesus

ner. There was, of course, the arranged murder of Bathsheba's husband so that David might possess the wife legally. Even more indicative of David's shrewd piety was his personal innocence combined with mafia-like politics whereby his relatives murdered opponents for him. He seized Jerusalem, a city that henceforth belonged to him and no tribe, and moved the Ark of the Covenant there to give the blessing of religion to his consolidation of power. Indeed, he succeeded in writing a codicil to God's covenant with His people. Now the covenant no longer simply stated: "You will be my people and I will be your God, if you keep my commandments"; it had an added condition: "and if you have a king of the house of David reigning over you" (see 2 Sam 7:24-26). All of this was combined with the sanctity of the sweet singer of psalms and originator of prayers so beautiful and profound that they have been the heart of divine praise, Jewish and monastic Christian, ever since.

This curious story of a Davidic monarchical institution that had divine origins but was frequently corrupt, venal, and uninspiring, was also part of "the story of the origin of Jesus Christ." Yes, that story involved not only individuals with their strengths and weaknesses like the patriarchs, but an institution, an organization, a structure, indeed a hierarchy (literally, in Greek, a sacred order) embodied in absolute rulers. I am not sure whether Zwingli would have been happy with that part of the story, but those of us who must be loyal both to the spontaneous grace of God and to a church with authority may get encouragement from this phase of Matthew's theology reflected in the incipient story of Jesus Christ.

THE UNKNOWN AND THE UNEXPECTED
If the "progress" from Abraham to the monarchy proved a mirage in the light of God's values, the last part of the genealogy from the deportation to Babylon to the divinely

Genealogy of Jesus

sent Christ or anointed king is more genuinely upbeat. It leads to the messianic savior of God's people. But what a curious cast of characters this more genuine progress involves. Except for the first two (Shealtiel and Zerubbabel) and the last two (Joseph and Mary), they are a collection of unknown people whose names never made it into sacred history for having done something significant. In other words, while powerful rulers in the monarchy brought God's people to a low point in recorded history (deportation), unknown people, presumably also proportionately divided among saints and sinners, were the vehicles of restoration. Still another indicator of the unpredictability of God's grace is that He accomplishes His purpose through those whom others regard as unimportant and forgettable.

Perhaps this is the moment to comment on the theological import of Matthew's including five women in the genealogy of Jesus Christ. In the light of Old Testament genealogies this is an unexpected item. Matthew's consistent ''A was the father of B'' pattern is not as male chauvinistic as it might seem if we remember that in the evangelist's view God was active in each begetting, so that biology is never the primary issue. It is refreshing, nevertheless, that Matthew took care to remind us explicitly that women as well as men were human components in Jesus' origins—a fitting reminder in a list that is described as ''a story of the *genesis* of Jesus Christ,'' evoking memories of an earlier Genesis story. The choice of the women who are mentioned is as surprising as the choice of many of the men. We hear nothing of the saintly patriarchal wives, Sarah, Rebekah, Rachel. Matthew begins rather with Tamar, a Canaanite outsider left childless by the death of her first and second husbands, both of them Judah's sons. When Judah failed to do his duty in providing her with a third son as husband, she disguised herself as a prostitute and seduced him. Only later when he found his widowed daughter-in-law in a pregnant situation that he

Genealogy of Jesus

regarded as disgraceful did she reveal that he was the father, causing Judah to recognize that she was more just and loyal to God's law then he was.[4] The next in the list is another outsider, the Canaanite Rahab—this time a real prostitute, but one whose kindness in protecting the Israelite spies made the conquest of Jericho possible (Joshua 2). Odd figures to be part of the beginning story of Jesus Christ, unless we remember his gracious dealings with sinners and prostitutes which were part of the story of his ministry. Ruth was another foreigner, a Moabite. Yet it was from her and not from her Israelite relatives that the impulse came to be faithful to the Law in raising up a child to her dead husband as she literally threw herself at the feet of Boaz. That child was to be the grandfather of David the king. The last Old Testament woman in the list is named by Matthew only through her pious husband Uriah, a Hittite, whom David had slain; she is Bathsheba, the victim of David's lust. The scandal of the affair and the loss of their love child did not discourage her from making certain that a second son, Solomon, succeeded David in the monarchy. All these women had a marital history that contained elements of human scandal or scorn; they were enterprising instruments, however, of God's spirit in continuing the sacred line of the Messiah. They fittingly introduce the fifth woman, Mary,[5] whose marital situation is also peculiar, since she is pregnant even though she has not had relations with her betrothed husband. Joseph is just or holy in his decision to divorce her, but divine revelation makes it clear that the last woman mentioned in the genealogy is more holy than he, for she is the instrument par excellence of the Holy Spirit who has begotten Jesus Christ in her womb.

[4]Although not included by Trible, this story borders on being a text of terror (footnote 3 above).

[5]The fact that the Old Testament women were foreigners does not prepare the way for Mary but prepares for Matthew's audience, which contained Gentile Christians along with Jewish ones (cf. Matt 10:5-6; 28:19).

Genealogy of Jesus

Looking back at the analysis of Matthew's genealogy that I have just given, we see how extraordinarily comprehensive is its theology of the roots of Jesus' story in the Old Testament. The genealogy is more than retrospective and instructive, however. We must recognize that in acting in Jesus Christ God is consistent with His action in Abraham and David, in the patriarchs, in the kings, and in the unknown. But that is only one aspect of the story of Jesus Christ, a story that has a sequence as well as a beginning; and the ongoing aspects are what makes the genealogy "good news" for Matthew's audience and for us. If the beginning of the story involved as many sinners as saints, so has the sequence. This means not simply a Peter who denied Jesus or a Paul who persecuted him, but sinners and saints among those who would bear his name throughout the ages. If we realize that human beings have been empowered to preserve, proclaim, and convey the salvation brought by Jesus Christ throughout ongoing history, the genealogy of the sequence of Jesus contains as peculiar an assortment of people as did the genealogy of the beginnings. The God who wrote the beginnings with crooked lines also writes the sequence with crooked lines, and some of those lines are our own lives and witness. A God who did not hesitate to use the scheming as well as the noble, the impure as well as the pure, men to whom the world hearkened and women upon whom the world frowned—this God continues to work through the same melange. If it was a challenge to recognize in the last part of Matthew's genealogy that totally unknown people were part of the story of Jesus Christ, it may be a greater challenge to recognize that the unknown characters of today are an essential part of the sequence. A sense of being unimportant and too insignificant to contribute to the continuation of the story of Jesus Christ in the world is belied by the genealogy, and the proclamation of that genealogy in the Advent liturgy is designed to give us hope about our destiny and our importance. The message of the genealogy is an enabling invitation.

Genealogy of Jesus

The genealogy has also taught us that God did not hesitate to entrust to a monarchical institution an essential role in the story of His Son's origins—an authoritative institution (at times authoritarian) which He guaranteed with promises lest it fail but which was frequently led by corrupt, venal, stupid, and ineffective leaders, as well as sometimes by saints. He has not hesitated to entrust the sequence of the story to a hierarchically structured church, guaranteed with promises, but not free from its own share of the corrupt, the venal, the stupid, and the ineffective. Those "Christians" who proclaim that they believe in and love Jesus but cannot accept the church or the institution because it is far from perfect and sometimes a scandal have not understood the beginning of the story and consequently are not willing to face the challenge of the sequence.

At the end of these comments let us return to the reference to Zwingli's approach mentioned at the beginning. By stressing the all-powerful grace of God, the genealogy presents its greatest challenge to those who will accept only an idealized Jesus Christ whose story they would write only with straight lines and whose portrait they would paint only in pastel colors. If we look at the whole story and the total picture, the genealogy teaches us that the beginning was not thus; the Gospels teach us that his ministry was not thus; the history of the church teaches us the sequence was not thus. That lesson is not a discouragement but an encouragement as we look forward to the liturgical coming of Christ. God's grace can work even with people like us. A meditation on "The story of the origin of Jesus Christ—Abraham fathered Isaac . . . Jesse fathered David the king . . . Achim fathered Eliud"—should convince reader and hearer that the authentic "story of the sequence of Jesus Christ" is that Jesus called Peter and Paul . . . Paul called Timothy . . . someone called you . . . and you must call someone else.

Genealogy of Jesus

Chapter 3

The Annunciation to Joseph (Matthew 1:18-25)

For most Christians "annunciation" automatically means the scene in Luke 1:26-38 where the Angel Gabriel appears to Mary at Nazareth to announce that she will conceive and bear a son to be called Jesus. Yet that is not the only annunciation of Jesus' birth. In Matthew's Infancy Narrative there is no annunciation to Mary; she remains a background figure. Rather there is an annunciation by an "angel of the Lord" to Joseph in a dream, telling him not to divorce Mary as he has planned, but to take her to his house, for her pregnancy is of the Holy Spirit. Matthew's annunciation may not have the poetic beauty of Luke's annunciation; one rarely if ever sees it portrayed in art. Yet it has its own dramatic force and theological insight, making it well worthy of proclamation as it occurs in the liturgy of the last week of Advent.

THE SETTING

In the genealogy that we have just discussed, i.e., the list of begettings that constitute the genesis or origin of Jesus Christ, Son of David, Son of Abraham (1:1), there is a set pattern (A was the father of B; B was the father of C) through three sets of fourteen generations. Yet when it comes to "the bottom line," to the generation that is the whole point of the genealogy, the format changes: not "Jacob was the father of Joseph, and Joseph was the father of Jesus who is called the Christ," but "Jacob was the father of Joseph, the husband of Mary, of whom was begotten Jesus, called the Christ." Subconsciously at least, the attentive reader of Matthew is bound to wonder about the peculiar phrasing. Matthew is going to explain that through his annunciation story, as he indicates in its opening line (1:18): "Now, as for Jesus Christ, his *genesis* [birth] took place in this way."[6] Christ or Messiah means "anointed one," and in particular the anointed king of the house of David. The genealogy has stressed the role of David the king, mentioning him more than anyone else (five times, 1:1, 6, 17); the annunciation will continue that theme since it is addressed to "Joseph, son of David." Although Matthew does not specifically localize the annunciation, in chapter 2 which follows the annunciation, we are told that Bethlehem was where Joseph and Mary had a home (2:11). It is fitting that Joseph, son of David, father of Jesus, Son of David, should live in Bethlehem, the place where David was born.

Nevertheless, the annunciation to Joseph not only looks back to and continues the themes of the genealogy; it looks forward to the rest of the Gospel. In that Gospel Matthew refers to Jesus as Son of David more often than do the other three Gospels taken together. Yet Matthew 22:41-46 makes it clear that Jesus is more than Son of David. He is decisively, by divine revelation, the Son of God (see 3:17; 16:16-17; 17:5). Accordingly, if the genealogy begins in 1:1 with the genesis of Jesus, Son of David, the annunciation will draw to an end in 1:23 describing the genesis of Emmanuel, "God with us."

Mary's strange pregnancy, which explains how Jesus is God with us, namely through the Holy Spirit, is another echo of the genealogy. As we saw in chapter 1, anomalously for genealogies, among Matthew's forty-two fathers (his count) were listed four Old Testament women, all of them with a history before marriage or childbirth that made their situation either strange or scandalous. In particular, Tamar, the widow of Judah's son, was found to be pregnant indecently long after her husband's death; Judah denounced her

---

[6]The double use of *genesis* in reference to Jesus Christ in 1:1 and 1:18 has a parallel in the double use of *genesis* in reference to Noah in Genesis 5:1; 6:9. Matthew is following Old Testament parallels very closely here.

Annunciation to Joseph

till he was made to realize that he was the father. Bathsheba, the wife of Uriah, became pregnant not by her husband but by David. Yet in all these instances the woman was God's instrument in preserving Israel and/or the lineage of the Messiah. So also, the fifth woman of the genealogy, Mary, is in a seemingly scandalous pregnancy. She and Joseph have been married,[7] but they are now in the customary interim period separating the marriage contract from the bride's living with the groom. Marriage, agreed upon by parents, usually came almost immediately after the age of puberty; but the girl continued to live with her parents for a time after the wedding until the husband was able to support her in his home or that of his parents. Marital intercourse was not permissible during that period;[8] yet Mary was now with child. What was Joseph to do?

THE DILEMMA OF A JUST MAN

A crucial verse in understanding the impact of the annunciation is Matthew 1:18-19: "Before they came together, Mary was found to be with child of the Holy Spirit; and Joseph her husband, being a just man and unwilling to shame her, decided to divorce her quietly." The logic of this description is not easy to discern. A popular view, especially among Roman Catholics, has interpreted the first clause literally, so that the discovery of Mary's pregnancy brought knowledge that it was through the efficacy of the Holy Spirit. Joseph's decision to divorce her stemmed from his awe or reverence for this divine intervention, of which he already knew when

[7]The verb in 1:18 is not the regular Greek verb "to marry"; evidently it was difficult to describe Jewish marriage customs in that language, even as it is in English. Nevertheless, translations such as "engage, betroth" do not do justice to the fact that the formal contract had been exchanged before witnesses and that Joseph is Mary's "husband" (1:16, 19).

[8]It is highly dubious whether reputed differences on this point between Galilee and Judea, suggested by later rabbinic references, were applicable at this time.

Annunciation to Joseph

the angel appeared to him. This knowledge gave him a sense of unworthiness in relation to Mary and an unwillingness to enter an ordinary marriage relationship with such an instrument of God. This interpretation is linguistically possible; it spares Joseph from ever having thought that Mary could behave shamefully.

For most scholars, however, this interpretation runs against the obvious flow of the narrative. Storywise, is it really plausible that the discovery that Mary was with child brought with it the knowledge that the pregnancy was of the Holy Spirit? Some interpreters argue that Matthew presupposed the Lucan annunciation where Mary learned of the overshadowing of the Holy Spirit and presumed that she had shared this knowledge along with the news of her pregnancy. But there is not an iota of evidence that Matthew or his readers knew of Luke's account. Similarly unrealistic is the thesis that Mary was so transparently holy that a knowledge of her pregnancy would bring the assumption that this was of God—we have no evidence that a virginal conception of the Messiah was expected in Judaism. Rather, as indicated above, the four Old Testament women mentioned in the genealogy prepare us for a seeming scandal in the fifth woman named in the Messiah's lineage. Matthew's statement that Mary "was found to be with child of the Holy Spirit" does not describe a knowledge that the finders had but a knowledge that the readers need, lest for a moment they think that the origin of Jesus Christ, in whom they believe, could have been scandalous.

That the dramatis personae in the story did *not* have a knowledge of the divine origin of Mary's child is the whole point of the angelic revelation to Joseph. The decision to divorce stems from Joseph's ignorance of the paternity; he is not the father, and he can only think that another is. When the angel says to him, "Do not fear to take Mary your wife to your home, for the child conceived in her is of the Holy

Annunciation to Joseph

30

Spirit," the angel is not telling Joseph something he already knows but something he needs to know. Patterned on angelic revelations to biblical fathers-to-be (see Abraham in Gen 17:15-22, and Zechariah in Luke 1:8-23), this is a communication of a divine plan for both the conception and the future of the infant.

Thinking Mary's pregnancy to be of human origin would not detract from Joseph's saintliness, unless one imposes on him a standard that would not be appropriate for a Jew of his time. Indeed, Matthew insists that Joseph was "just" (or "upright" or "righteous"), a designation that implies conformity to the Law of God, the supreme Jewish standard of holiness. (Compare the same adjective applied to Zechariah and Elizabeth in Luke 1:6: "They were both righteous before God, walking blamelessly in all the commandments and ordinances of the Lord.") Mary should have come to Joseph a virgin, and now she was with child. His decision to divorce her showed a sensitivity to Israel's understanding of the sanctity of marriage required by God's Law, since her loss of virginity might have been considered adultery (Deut 22:20-21).[9] But Joseph was also sensitive to the protective character of the Law, which indicated two ways in which a woman might become pregnant before joining her husband: she might willingly have relations with another and commit adultery (Deut 22:20-24), or she might be forced against her will and thus remain innocent (Deut 22:25-27). To determine Mary's complicity or innocence and the treatment to which she might be subject, Joseph could have demanded a trial (and presumably have escaped returning the dowry if she were guilty). Joseph, however, did not manifest his righteousness at Mary's expense: "He was unwilling to expose

---

[9]A second-century Christian interpretation of the scene is found in the *Protevangelium of James* 14:1: "If I hide her sin, I am fighting the Law of the Lord." Justin Martyr, Augustine, and Chrysostom all understood that Joseph was being obedient to the law.

Annunciation to Joseph

her to public disgrace" or "to make a public spectacle of her" (two precise translations of the Greek verb involved in 1:19). Accordingly, Joseph was going to divorce her "quietly"—not in the sense that no one would know of it, but in the sense that there would be no formal inquiry into Mary's behavior.

In my judgment, this understanding of the justice of Joseph, rather than the "awe" or "reverence" explanation mentioned above, is essential to Matthew's picture of Christianity. In the next chapter Matthew will describe Gentile magi coming to worship the King of the Jews guided by divine revelation through the star, while Jewish leaders who have more precise revelation available in the Scriptures (Herod, the chief priests, and the scribes) seek to kill him— note the plural in 2:20: "Those who sought the child's life." One might falsely assume that in Matthew's dualistic view there are only good Gentiles and bad Jews. Rather, the hero of Matthew's infancy story is Joseph, a very sensitive Jewish observer of the Law, who is brought through God's revelation to accept Jesus, saving him from destruction. For Matthew it was perfectly possible to be simultaneously a Law-observant Jew and a Christian, since Jesus proclaimed that every jot and tittle of the Law would be preserved (5:18), praised those who kept even the least commandments (5:19), and appreciated scribes who could treasure what is new along with what is old (13:52). Such Law-observant, believing Jews preserved the memory of Jesus and through their proclamation made disciples of the Gentiles (28:19). Thus, in Joseph, the evangelist was portraying what he thought a Jew should be and probably what he himself was.

In the proclamation of the annunciation scene, this point is worth developing. There is a poignancy in Matthew's Joseph, righteously concerned for the Law of God, but seeking also to prevent Mary's public disgrace. Obviously, Matthew's story may imply Joseph's love for his bride, but we should

Annunciation to Joseph

not contrast too simply obedience to the Law and love as the opposing motives in his behavior. Rather, Joseph understands that the Law in all its complexity allows behavior that is sensitive, neither assuming the worst nor seeking the maximum punishment. That is why Matthew can reconcile a profound obedience to the Law with an acceptance of Jesus. His objection to the legalists is not that they keep God's law exactly, but that they do not understand the depth of God's purpose in the Law. In 12:1-8 he will describe Jesus as the Lord of the Sabbath, accused of condoning violations of the Law, but truly perceptive as to how God has acted in past applications of the Law. In the church of our own times where a mention of law may evoke legalism (either because of past memories or because of unimaginative enforcement by those who should be interpreting), Matthew's sensitive description of a Law-obedient or righteous Joseph may give new import to the invocation "St. Joseph."

THE "HOW" OF JESUS' IDENTITY

That Joseph should not divorce Mary was crucial in God's plan, not primarily for the sake of Mary's reputation, but for Jesus' identity. The child must be the son of Joseph, the son of David, thus fulfilling God's promise to David, "I will raise up your son after you. . . . I will make his royal throne firm forever" (2 Sam 7:12-13). The angel points to this essential element by addressing Joseph as "Son of David." Yet the most frequent question asked by modern readers is: "How can Jesus be Joseph's son if Joseph did not beget him?" Evidently, this issue disturbed Gentiles in antiquity as well, for soon it was being claimed that Mary was of the house of David, presumably in an attempt to trace Jesus' Davidic line through her. But for Judaism, as the genealogy indicates, the royal lineage of the Messiah had to be traced through a series of fathers to David. Matthew gives the answer to the modern question when Joseph is told, "She is to bear a son,

Annunciation to Joseph

and *you* are to name him Jesus.'' Judaism wrestled with the fact that it is easy to tell who is a child's mother, but difficult to tell who is a child's father. To establish paternity, it is not sufficient to ask the wife because she might lie about the father in order to avoid being accused of adultery. Rather the husband should give testimony since most men are reluctant to acknowledge a child unless it is their own. The Mishna *Baba Bathra* (8:6), written some 200 years after Jesus' birth, is lucidly clear: ''If a man says, 'This is my son,' he is to be believed.'' Joseph gives such an acknowledgment by naming the child; thus he becomes the legal father of Jesus. (This is a more correct description than adoptive father or foster father.) The identity of Jesus as Son of David is in God's plan, but Joseph must give to that plan a cooperative obedience that befits a righteous man.

The name that Joseph is to give the child is Jesus ''because he will save his people from their sins.'' The sequence in chapter 2 of Matthew will show how this New Testament Joseph, who receives revelation in dreams and goes to Egypt to save the infant, is reliving the great epic of the Old Testament figure named Joseph who interpreted dreams and went to Egypt, thereby saving Israel/Jacob (Gen 45:5; 50:20). That Genesis epic is continued in Exodus by the story of Moses: he escaped as an infant from the wicked pharaoh who killed male children and then returned after those who sought his life were dead (Exod 2:1-10; 4:19). Similarly, with Joseph's help, the infant Jesus escapes the wicked Herod who killed male children and is brought back to Palestine after those who sought his life are dead.[10] The name Jesus fits into this parallelism between the Matthew story of Joseph and the Old Testament story of Joseph and Moses, for Moses' successor who completed his work by bringing Israel back to the Promised Land was also named Jesus (Joshua). In reference to the latter, the Jewish philosopher Philo, who lived in New

[10]Matthew 2:20 is a literal echo of Exodus 4:19.

Annunciation to Joseph

34

Testament times, explains: "Jesus is interpreted 'salvation of the Lord'—a name for the best possible state." But Matthew's explanation of the name goes beyond this basic idea of salvation: "You shall call his name Jesus, for he will save *his people* from their sins." The latter clause is also an echo of the Moses' story; for the first-century A.D. Jewish historian Josephus in his *Antiquities* (2.9.3; #216) relates that in a dream God told Moses' father that the child about to be born would ultimately "deliver the Hebrew race from their bondage in Egypt." Both Moses and Jesus are saviors of their people, but in Matthew's understanding the people of Jesus would be not only the Jewish descendants of Moses' Hebrews but all the nations (28:19). The bondage is no longer that of Egypt but of sin.

Matthew has now told us that the child in Mary's womb will through Joseph's naming be Son of David and the savior of his people. Yet there is a greater identity which Joseph must accept, but to which he cannot contribute: the child will be Emmanuel, "God with us," because Mary has conceived him through the Holy Spirit. Matthew has nothing of Luke's elaboration of this element in the annunciation to Mary (Luke 1:35): "The Holy Spirit will come upon you; the power of the Most High will overshadow you; therefore the one to be born will be called holy, Son of God." Yet the fact that the two different accounts mention conception through the Holy Spirit rather than through male generation[11] suggests that this is a most ancient phrasing, antedating both evangelists and coming from Christian tradition. The New Testament indicates clearly that the awesome, creative, life-giving power of the Spirit was associated with the resurrection of Jesus— God's Son who was enabled to conquer death dispenses the Spirit enabling believers to become God's children. In the

[11]While both evangelists think that Jesus was conceived without a human father, neither concentrates on the biological aspect; the christological revelation of Jesus' identity is their concern.

Annunciation to Joseph

Gospels the Spirit is primarily associated with the baptism of Jesus as he begins his public life of proclaiming the kingdom. But in the two Infancy Narratives it is related to the very beginning of Jesus' life: he is so much God's Son that God is his only Father, not through sexual intervention but through the same power of the Spirit that brought life into the world at the creation. If the genealogy of Matthew takes the story of Jesus back to Abraham, implicitly the virginal conception finds an analogy further back with Adam, the other human being whose life did not come from human generation.

In order to explain to his readers the full import of this generation by the Spirit announced in 1:20-21 ("It is by the Holy Spirit she has conceived this child; she will bear a son"), Matthew in the subsequent verses turns to the prophet Isaiah (7:14): "Behold the virgin will be with child and will give birth to a son, and they will call his name Emmanuel." Thus, there is a second name for the child beyond that of Jesus Son of David, the savior of his people; he is Emmanuel, "God with us." If this name comes through begetting by the Holy Spirit, we are not surprised in finding the name related to the postresurrectional setting in which that Spirit functions. The risen Jesus' last words in Matthew (28:20) are, "I am *with you* always to the end of the world." The enduring presence of God's Spirit in the risen Jesus was already a reality at the conception of Jesus; what was made known by angelic revelation to Joseph, the just Jew, would be made known to all the nations until the end of the world by the apostolic preaching and teaching.

Matthew clearly rejoices to find that what God speaks through the angel fulfills what He had already spoken through the prophet. We have emphasized Matthew's sense of continuity with Israel: the names in the genealogy show a continuity with the Law and the Former Prophets (that is, those Books of the Old Testament that we call the Pentateuch and Historical Books, extending from Genesis to the end of

Annunciation to Joseph

Kings). But the corpus of the Latter Prophets (that is, the works of the Writing Prophets) bears preeminent witness to God's plan. In chapter 2 Matthew will quote these Latter Prophets four times (Micah, Hosea, Jeremiah, and presumably Isaiah) as having referred to the places where the Messiah would accomplish his task. In this chapter, Matthew begins with a quote from Isaiah 7:14 about the Messiah's origin. He does not necessarily mean that the prophets themselves foresaw Jesus,[12] but through their words Matthew sees the divine plan. In these various quotations, Matthew's wording tends to be closer to the Greek translation of the Jewish Scriptures, known to us as the Septuagint, than to the wording of the Hebrew text—not illogically since he is writing for Greek speakers. Yet often, as here, Matthew agrees verbatim with neither Hebrew nor Greek. (In his rendering of Isaiah 7:14, the "virgin" and the future tenses agree with the Greek; the "be with child" is closer to the Hebrew; the "they will call" agrees with neither.) The evangelist's ability to move back and forth among the variants of the Scriptures has caused some to think of a Matthean school; at least such technical ability may be the mark of a scribe trained for the kingdom of heaven (13:52). To the modern mind, Matthew seems almost dishonest in picking wording that best suits his application, even to the point of adjusting the scriptural wording for a better fit.[13] But that attitude mistakenly assumes that Matthew is interpreting the Scriptures to explain Jesus, even as the Dead Sea Essenes strove to throw light on their present situation by writing

[12]Some moderns are far more literalist in their hermeneutics than were the Jews of Jesus' time. The Dead Sea Essenes stated explicitly that the full meaning of their words lay beyond the comprehension of the prophets.

[13]Besides the observations made above, it should be noted that at this time, while there were sacred writings or books, there was not yet in regard to many books one fixed form of the text that was regarded as sacred. Evidently the Dead Scroll group was not bothered to have the members using copies of Isaiah, for example, that had very different readings and spellings.

Annunciation to Joseph

commentaries on the Old Testament Books line-by-line, word-by-word. The fact that no such commentary exists in the New Testament suggests that the process was the other way around: Christians interpreted Jesus who cast light on the Scriptures. The technical hermeneutical procedures were often the same whether used by Jews or by Jewish believers in Jesus, but for the latter the hermeneutical focus was different. For them the revelation in Jesus was the supreme authority even over the Scriptures.

Scholars point out that Isaiah 7:14 was addressed by the prophet to King Ahaz of Judah about an event soon to occur in Isaiah's time, over seven hundred years before Christ. But they sometimes miss the exact words of Isaiah's address which would have influenced Matthew's approach. In 7:13, the prophet speaks to the king not by personal name but as "House of David." Thus the second identity of Jesus as Emmanuel, "God with us," made evident in Isaiah, is not unrelated to the first identity as "Son of David." The prophet's words are appropriately placed by Matthew after a genealogy that led from David the King through the descendants of his house to Joseph son of David, "husband of Mary of whom was begotten Jesus, called the Christ." Matthew's insistence that "*they* will call his name Emmanuel," rather than the "she will call" of Isaiah's Hebrew or the "you will call" of the Greek rendition of Isaiah, opens the reader's vision to a wider audience, namely, the "his people" whom he saves from sin—not only those who accepted the Davidic lineage in Judea, but the nations of the world. In the chapter immediately following, those nations of the world will begin to make their appearance through their representatives, the magi from the East.

Matthew ends the annunciation with an emphasis on Joseph's compliance illustrating the extent to which he is truly just or righteous. Joseph completed the second stage of his marriage to Mary by taking his wife to his home; and he

Annunciation to Joseph

named the child Jesus, thus acknowledging his son—the two specific commands of the angel. But Joseph went beyond the angel's command in order to fulfill the prophet's word. The angel had told Joseph that the child in Mary's womb was of the Holy Spirit, thus matching the first clause of Isaiah: "The virgin shall conceive." The prophet continued by affirming that the virgin would "bear a son"; and so we are told explicitly by Matthew that Joseph did not know Mary until she bore a son. This is Matthew's affirmation that Mary not only conceived as a virgin but remained a virgin until she gave birth. Unfortunately, some modern polemics have obscured the import of what Matthew was telling us by assuming that he was giving information implicitly about what happened after birth. Whether or not he had such information, he was not indicating it even implicitly here; his concern was with the fulfillment of the prophetic past rather than Christian disputes of subsequent centuries. Matthew's concern was with a Joseph who fulfilled every jot and tittle of the Law and the Prophets, worthily serving as a father to a son who would insist on the fulfillment of the Law and the Prophets. Concentration on that image of Joseph should be the real concern of Christians who claim to be loyal to the Scriptures.

Annunciation to Joseph

Chapter 4

The Annunciation to Zechariah and the Birth of the Baptist (Luke 1:5-25, 57-66, 80)

Thus far we have reflected on the two scenes that constitute chapter 1 of Matthew—scenes with which the church's liturgy begins the last week of the Advent season (December 17-23). We now turn to Luke's much longer chapter 1 with which the liturgy continues the rest of the days of that week. This chapter tells us a very different story from Matthew's chapter, alike in only a few (but very important) details, namely, that an angel announced that Mary, who was married to Joseph of the house of David, would give birth to a child conceived through the Holy Spirit and that child, the Son of God, should be named Jesus. Even in these similarities there is a major difference: the angel in Luke announces to Mary, not to Joseph as in Matthew. The rest of Luke's narrative and Luke's cast of characters is very different from Matthew's. Luke tells us of the annunciation to Zechariah informing him that his wife Elizabeth would give birth to John the Baptist, of the visitation of Mary to Elizabeth which occasions the Magnificat, and of the birth of the Baptist which occasions the Benedictus.

Yet in basic motifs and theology Matthew and Luke are quite similar despite the different stories they tell. Matthew's genealogy, which has "the origin of Jesus Christ" begin with Abraham fathering Isaac, has shown us that the story of God's action in Israel may be seen as part of the story of Jesus. Matthew's annunciation to Joseph combines clear echoes of Old Testament patriarchal stories with New Testament "good news" that Jesus is not only the Messiah of the house of David but the presence of God among us. The believing acceptance of this by Joseph, the just man, illustrates how faith was combined with observance of the Law by the believing Jews who were the first to hear the good news. All these motifs will reappear, even if in a different guise, in Luke 1. Each of the two evangelists in his own way has preserved for us from very early Christian tradition insights about God's preparation for His Messiah and Son, insights that are still an essential part of the church's Advent preparation.

LUCAN STRUCTURE AND THE FUNCTION OF CHAPTER 1

To appreciate how Luke uses the annunciation of the Baptist's birth to prepare for Jesus' birth, one must first appreciate the role of the Infancy Narrative in the overall structure of Lucan theology; for Luke is a writer who uses structure artistically to convey his thought. No Gospel begins the story of Jesus' public ministry without telling the reader of John the Baptist. Evidently the Baptist's preceding Jesus was fixed in Christian tradition, indeed so irradicably fixed that in two of the three Gospels that begin their story before the public ministry with Jesus' first appearance on earth, the Baptist is brought back to precede that appearance as well. In John's Prologue before the light comes into the world we hear that "There was sent by God a man named John." In Luke not only does the annunciation of the Baptist's conception precede that of Jesus but the Baptist's birth (hailed by Zechariah's canticle) precedes Jesus' birth (hailed by Simeon's canticle). This carefully crafted parallelism has often been compared to a diptych painting with its two facing panels.

Luke's activity, however, goes beyond the Baptist-Jesus parallelism. His architectonic perception of God's plan divides all history into three parts: the time of the Law and the Prophets, the time of Jesus, and the time of the church—a triptych this time. Jesus is the centerpiece; beforehand the Law and the Prophets bear witness to him (Acts 13:14); afterwards the Spirit and those whom Jesus has chosen bear wit-

Annunciation to Zechariah and Birth of the Baptist

ness to him (Acts 1:9). The time of the Law and the Prophets is the period that Christians associate with the Old Testament. The time of Jesus runs from the baptism to the ascension (Acts 1:21-22) and is the subject of the Gospel proper. The two are connected by the Infancy Narratives in Luke 1-2, the bridge chapters that open the Gospel. The time of the church's bearing witness to Jesus runs from after the coming of the Spirit at Pentecost until the message reaches the ends of the earth (Acts 1:8). The time of Jesus and the time of the church are connected by the reappearance of Jesus (who ascended on Easter Sunday night in Luke 24:51) to instruct those whom he has chosen; this is described in Acts 1-2, the bridge chapters that open Luke's second book. Both the "bridge" sections (Luke 1-2; Acts 1-2) have similar features: they begin in Jerusalem; revelation comes from heaven in extraordinary ways; the earthly participants break forth in eloquent prophecy, as God dramatizes the coming of the Son and the coming of the Spirit. In both, characters from the material that precedes encounter characters from the material that is to follow, i.e., in Luke 1-2 characters and motifs from the Law and the Prophets encounter characters from the Gospel account of the ministry (John the Baptist and Mary); in Acts 1-2 the Jesus of the Gospel encounters the Twelve, including Peter, who are to proclaim him to the ends of the earth.

Drawing from this structure and confining ourselves to the Lucan infancy chapters, we can see that Luke's technique, while different from Matthew's, accomplishes much the same purpose. Matthew opens his first chapter with "Abraham was the father of Isaac"; as we shall see, Luke opens his first chapter with a description of Zechariah, the father of the Baptist as an Abraham-like figure. Both rehearse the story of Israel even though they choose different moments in that story to emphasize. And both anticipate the essential gospel message.

Annunciation to Zechariah and Birth of the Baptist

Luke begins the annunciation of the Baptist's coming by introducing the principal human agents in the conception, Zechariah and Elizabeth, impeccably upright or just figures, even as Matthew's annunciation (1:19) described Joseph as upright or just. No other New Testament author even mentions the Baptist's parents or suggests that he was the son of a priest, or related to Jesus. While for some of these details Luke may be drawing on historical tradition, he is primarily interested in the symbolism of what he narrates. Several Old Testament parents were barren but made capable of childbearing by divine intervention, even as Elizabeth is; but in only one Old Testament instance were both parents also incapacitated by age, as Zechariah and Elizabeth are, namely, Abraham and Sarah, so prominent in Genesis, the first book of the Law. That Luke intends a parallelism between the two sets of parents is made clear by Zechariah's response to the angel after hearing the news of the conception: "How am I to know this?" (Luke 1:18), a verbatim quotation from Abraham's response to divine revelation in Genesis 15:8. Also Elizabeth's rejoicing with her neighbors who hear the good news (1:58) echoes Sarah's rejoicing with all who hear her good news (Gen 21:6).

Luke's artistry goes farther, however. Zechariah and Elizabeth are portrayed as similar to another pair of Old Testament parents whose yearning for a child was answered by God, namely, Elkanah and Hannah, the parents of Samuel. Indeed the opening of the Lucan story in 1:5, "There was a certain priest named Zechariah . . . he had a wife . . . and her name was Elizabeth," reminds us strongly of the opening of 1 Samuel 1:1-2: "There was a certain man . . . whose name was Elkanah . . . and he had two wives; the name of one was Hannah." The revelation to Hannah that she would give birth to Samuel came through the priest Eli during the annual visit to the sanctuary to offer sacrifice (1

Annunciation to Zechariah and Birth of the Baptist

Sam 1:3, 17), even as the forthcoming birth is revealed to the priest Zechariah in the sanctuary of the Jerusalem Temple. In both stories the child to be born would drink neither wine nor strong drink (Luke 1:15; 1 Sam 1:9-15) and thus be a Nazirite dedicated to the Lord (Nm 6:1-21). The Magnificat of Luke 1:46-55 is strongly evocative of Hannah's canticle of 1 Samuel 2:1-10.[14] If the story of Abraham and Sarah belongs to the Law, the story of Samuel belongs to the Prophets.[15] Reminiscences of the Law (Leviticus) are again found in the setting of the annunciation of the Baptist's conception, namely, the priestly offering of incense; and the prophetic theme is continued when Zechariah speaks prophetically in Luke 1:67, and implicitly in the description of the future Baptist as Elijah in 1:17, which echoes Malachi 3:1, 23-24 (RSV 3:1; 4:5-6), the last of the prophetic writings.

The Lucan technique of echoing the Scriptures of Israel is continued even more dramatically in the appearance of the angel who identifies himself as Gabriel. After the Law and the Prophets in the collection of canonical Scriptures come the Writings, one of which was the Book of Daniel.[16] Only in that Old Testament book does Gabriel make an appearance. In both Luke (1:22) and Daniel (six times in chapters 9-10) the appearance is called a vision. In both (Luke 1:10-11, Dan 9:20-21) Gabriel comes at the time of liturgical prayer to a figure who has been praying in distress (Luke 1:13; Dan 9:20). In both the visionary becomes afraid, is told not to fear, and eventually is struck mute (Luke 1:12-13, 20, 22; Dan 10:8, 12, 15). There can be little doubt, then, that Luke intends us to

[14]The parallelism to the Samuel story is continued in Luke 2 as Jesus is presented in the Temple and in the greeting given him by a figure named Hannah/Anna.

[15]Most of the "Historical Books" of the Christian Bible were considered "Former Prophets" in Jewish terminology.

[16]In the Hebrew Scriptures, unlike the Christian Old Testament, Daniel is not classified as a Book of Prophecy. Luke 24:44 shows consciousness of further writings beyond the Law and the Prophets.

Annunciation to Zechariah and Birth of the Baptist

see a parallelism between Gabriel's appearance to Daniel and his appearance to Zechariah. We have seen Zechariah described in language reminiscent of Abraham, the first of the patriarchs, who is described in the first book of the Hebrew Scriptures. Now he encounters Gabriel, the angel of the endtime, who interprets the seventy weeks of years—that panoramic description of God's final plan in the last part of which "everlasting justice will be introduced, vision and prophecy will be ratified, and a Holy of Holies will be anointed." (Luke probably understood the Greek of this last phrase in Daniel 9:24 in terms of a *christos*, an anointed one or messiah.) Gabriel is described in a book that belongs to the last portion of the Hebrew Scriptures and indeed, perhaps, was the last book of the collection to be written. Matthew may be more methodical in his genealogy by proceeding from Abraham to the time of the Messiah, but in his allusive way Luke has covered the same span in this encounter between Zechariah/Abraham and Gabriel, the final messenger who brings the years of history to a close. Both authors have covered the span of God's dealing with Israel down to the last times.

The child to be born is an appropriate figure in this eschatological context: John the Baptist who "will go before the Lord in the spirit and power of Elijah to turn the hearts of the fathers to the children . . . to make ready for the Lord a prepared people." Luke (16:16) expresses his view of the Baptist in a famous saying of Jesus: "The Law and the Prophets were until John; since then the kingdom of God is preached." We have seen that these infancy chapters of Luke are a bridge between the time of the Law and the Prophets and the time of Jesus' proclamation of the kingdom. As part of that bridge the Baptist's parents, parallel to Abraham and Sarah and to the parents of Samuel, belong to the Law and the Prophets, observing all the commandments and ordinances of the Law (1:6) and prophesying themselves (1:41,

Annunciation to Zechariah and Birth of the Baptist

45

67). But the Baptist belongs to the time of Jesus. Consequently, the child is described in language anticipatory of the
descriptions of him found in the Gospel accounts of Jesus'
public ministry. Indeed the communication about his conception is described as proclaiming the good news or gospel in
1:19. If Luke 1:15a promises that the Baptist "will be great,"
this anticipates Jesus' description of him in Luke 7:28,
"Among those born of women, none is greater than John."
That the child will be "before the Lord" (1:15b) anticipates
7:27, "Behold, I send my messenger before your face who
will prepare your way ahead of you" (even if the Greek
vocabulary differs slightly). The prediction in 1:15b that the
Baptist "will drink no wine or strong drink" is an adaptation
of the tradition in 7:33: "John the Baptist has come eating no
bread and drinking no wine." The promise that the child
"will be filled with the Holy Spirit even from his mother's
womb" is the initial step of what will culminate in 3:2: "The
word of God came to John, the son of Zechariah, in the desert." (To appreciate the full force of the two descriptions one
should compare the alternation of spirit and word in biblical
vocations, e.g., Isa 61:1 and 2:1; Joel 3:1 [RSV 2:28] and 1:1.)[17]
In short, Luke knows of the Baptist from the traditions of
Jesus' ministry, and he has anticipated this information in
the annunciation of the conception of the Baptist. This illustrates my contention that in the Lucan Infancy Narratives
there are Old Testament figures (Zechariah and Elizabeth)
and Gospel figures (the Baptist) encountering each other in
order to bridge the two periods of God's salvific action.

The immediate aftermath of the annunciation draws out
farther the symbolism of that scene. We are told that, struck
mute (like Daniel), Zechariah went to his home and after-

[17]The promise that the Baptist will "turn the hearts of the fathers to the
children" quotes the description of Elijah in Malachi 3:24 (RSV 4:6), but it
may have been influenced by Gospel sayings pertinent to the Baptist which
speak of father and/or children (Luke 3:8; 7:31-33).

Annunciation to Zechariah and Birth of the Baptist

46

wards Elizabeth conceived, a description that echoes the behavior of the parents of Samuel: "Then they went to their
home . . . and in due time Hannah conceived" (1 Sam
1:19-20). Elizabeth's reaction (Luke 1:25), "The Lord has dealt
with me in this way," is reminiscent of 1 Samuel's description of Hannah: "The Lord remembered her." The taking
away of Elizabeth's "disgrace" reminds us of Rachel's reaction to conception in Genesis 30:23, "God has taken away my
disgrace." (The visitation of Mary to Elizabeth and
Elizabeth's praise of Mary really belong more to the annunciation of the conception of Jesus and will be discussed in relation to that scene.) The actual birth of the Baptist is described
by Luke with surprising brevity in 1:57-58. The rejoicing of
the neighbors when they hear echoes the rejoicing of all who
hear of Sarah's giving birth (Gen 21:6).

More attention is concentrated on the naming of the Baptist. Zechariah had been struck mute following the angel's
annunciation because he had not believed (1:20); now his
obedience in wanting the child to be named John as the angel commissioned shows that indeed he has believed; consequently, his muteness is relieved. The marvelous coincidence
that Elizabeth also chooses the name John, even though there
is no one in the family with that name, is a further sign that
the hand of the Lord was with the child (1:66). The miracle,
like the miracles of Jesus in the ministry, provokes awe and
wonder. The statement that "as the child grew up, he became strong in spirit" (1:80) and "the hand of the Lord was
with him" (1:66) are final reminiscences of the Abraham-
Sarah and the parents-of-Samuel stories. After the birth and
circumcision of Isaac, the child born to Abraham and Sarah,
we are told, "The child grew up" (Gen 21:8), and of Samuel
we hear "The child grew strong before the Lord" (1 Sam
2:21).[18] The last sentence of this chapter (Luke 1:80), "He

[18]See also the Samson story in Judges 13:24-25 (Greek): "The child became
mature and the Lord blessed him, and the Spirit of the Lord began to go
with him."

Annunciation to Zechariah and Birth of the Baptist

47

stayed in the desert until the day of his public appearance to Israel,'' is Luke's final artistic touch in developing the bridge aspect of the story—it connects to 3:2, ''The word of God came to John, the son of Zechariah, in the desert.''

Thus far there has been nothing said about Zechariah's canticle, the Benedictus. I shall devote the next essay to that magnificent poem and to the Lucan canticles in general.

Annunciation to Zechariah and Birth of the Baptist

Chapter 5

The Benedictus (Luke 1:67-79)

In the Lucan Infancy Narrative there are four canticles (hymns or psalms): in chapter one, the Benedictus and the Magnificat, which are read in the Gospels of the last week of Advent; in chapter 2 the Gloria in Excelsis and the Nunc Dimittis, which are read in the Gospels of the Christmas season. Of course, the church's liturgical use of these canticles is far wider since three of them are prominent in the daily Divine Office, and an expanded form of the Gloria is part of the Mass. For that reason let me comment in general on all four before I turn to the Benedictus. While I shall treat them together, the Gloria is so brief that only by analogy can we guess that its origin may be the same as that of the others. Let me note, however, the fact that the Gloria is spoken by angels while the others are spoken by human beings is not an important difference. The Gloria may have been structured antiphonally, with one set of lines now assigned to the angels:

"Glory in the highest heavens to God,
and on earth peace to those favored (by Him),"

while the other set of lines was assigned to the disciples as Jesus enters Jerusalem in Luke 19:38:

"Peace in heaven,
and glory in the highest heavens."

THE ORIGIN OF THE LUCAN CANTICLES

Although in the Infancy Narrative Luke has various characters speak these canticles, modern scholarship has moved away from thinking that they were respectively the historical compositions of Mary, Zechariah, or Simeon (or, a fortiori, of angels). They have an overall common style and a poetic polish that militate against such individual, on-the-spot composi-

The Benedictus

tion. Indeed, in several of the canticles there are individual lines that do not fit the situation of the putative spokesperson. For example, how has Mary's conception "scattered the proud in the imagination of their hearts," "filled the hungry with good things," and "sent the rich away empty" (lines from the Magnificat)? How does the birth of the Baptist constitute "salvation from our enemies and from the hand of all those who hate us" (Benedictus)? Accordingly most scholars think that the canticles had a common origin and were adapted and inserted into the Infancy Narrative.

Some think that the evangelist himself composed them, but then one might have expected a greater uniformity among the canticles and a smoother fit into their present context. (If the Magnificat, Benedictus, and Nunc Dimittis [and the line that leads into each] were omitted from their present context, no one would even suspect that there was anything missing.[19]) More scholars, therefore, think that substantially the canticles came from a preLucan source and were taken over by the evangelist and inserted into their present places. I say "substantially" because there are Lucan additions to make them fit their context. For instance, Luke may have added 1:48 to the Magnificat,

"Because He has regarded the low estate of His handmaid—
for behold, henceforth all generations will call me fortunate."

That verse echoes language that Luke has already used of Mary in 1:38, 42, and thus helps to make the canticle appropriate on her lips. Similarly in the Benedictus verses 76–77 may well be a Lucan addition to make the canticle appropriate to the birth of John the Baptist (cf. Luke 1:17; 3:4; 7:27):

"But you, child, will be prophet of the Most High,
for you will go before the Lord to make ready His ways,
to grant His people knowledge of salvation
in the forgiveness of their sins."

[19]For instance, 1:56 reads very smoothly following 1:45; 1:80 smoothly following 1:66. Greater effort was made by the evangelist in incorporating the canticles of chapter 2 in the flow of the narrative.

The Benedictus

What was the source from which Luke drew these canticles if he did not compose them himself? There is no doubt whatever that they represent Jewish hymnic style and thought of the general period from 200 B.C. to A.D. 100, as illustrated in 1 Maccabees, Judith, 2 *Baruch*, 4 *Ezra*, and the Dead Sea (Qumran) *War Scroll* and *Thanksgiving Psalms*. The dominant stylistic pattern is that of a cento or mosaic pattern where almost every phrase and line is taken from the earlier poetry of Israel, i.e., the Psalms, the Prophets, and hymns in the Pentateuch and the Historical Books. In my *Birth of the Messiah* (Garden City: Doubleday, 1977) I supplied whole pages of Old Testament poetic background for each line of the Magnificat (358–60), the Benedictus (386–89), and the Nunc Dimittis (458). Let me give one illustration here from the opening of the Benedictus (Luke 1:68-69):

> "Blessed be the Lord, the God of Israel,
>   because He has visited
>   and accomplished the redemption of His people,
>   and has raised up for us a horn of salvation
>   in the house of David His servant."

In Psalm 41:14(13) and in other psalm passages we find: "Blessed be the Lord, the God of Israel." Psalm 111:9 says that God "sent redemption to His people," while Judges 3:9 states, "The Lord raised up a Saviour for Israel." Psalm 132:17 has God saying, "I shall make a horn to sprout for David," a statement similar to the motif in Ezekiel 29:21: "On that day I shall make a horn sprout for all the house of Israel." In a Jewish prayer contemporary with the Lucan Benedictus (the Fifteenth Benediction of the *Shemoneh Esreh*) we find a similar mosaic, "Let the shoot of David (Your servant) speedily spring up and raise his horn in Your salvation. . . . May you be blessed, O Lord, who lets the horn of salvation flourish."

So Jewish are the Lucan canticles that some scholars have thought that the evangelist took them over from a collection

The Benedictus

that had nothing to do with Jesus Christ. There is, however, a particular tone of divine salvation *accomplished* and (in the Benedictus) an emphasis on the house of David that would not be readily explicable from the non-Christian Jewish history of this period. The non-Christian Jewish hymns that offer the best parallels to the Benedictus and the Magnificat are prayers yearning for salvation. True, the Maccabean victories of the second century B.C. might have prompted songs of deliverance, but that deliverance would not be described as Davidic, for the Maccabee leaders were levitical priests. Thus the probability is that we are dealing with Jewish Christian hymns celebrating the salvific action of God in Jesus, the Messiah.

Indeed, the tendency has been to speak of the hymns of a Jewish-Christian *community;* for, despite the overall similar style, there are enough differences among the canticles to make us posit different authors with the same background. The "we" of the Benedictus and the latter part of the Magnificat ("our fathers") reflect the spokespersons of a collectivity. More particularly attempts have been made to derive the canticles from a group within Israel of Christian "Poor Ones" *(Anawim):* those who, in part, were physically poor but more widely would not trust their own strength and had to rely totally on God for deliverance—the lowly, the sick, the downtrodden. Their praises are sung in Psalm 149:4: "The Lord takes pleasure in His people; He adorns the Poor Ones with victory." Certainly the Dead Sea *Thanksgiving Hymns* have this ambiance, "You, O Lord, have assisted the soul of the Poor Ones and the needy against one who is strong. You have redeemed my soul from the hand of the mighty." The Magnificat, in particular, would fit such a background, with its lines, "He has exalted those of low degree; He has filled the hungry with good things."

This proposed background has been made even more specific by those scholars who think of a community of Jewish

The Benedictus

Christian Poor Ones *at Jerusalem*. In Acts 2:43-47; 4:32-37, Luke pays particular attention to the first Jewish believers in Jesus in that city, describing them as people who sold their possessions and gave their wealth to be distributed to the needy. His description of these Poor Ones borders on nostalgia and may well be idealized, but Paul's collection of money for the Jerusalem church, often mentioned in his letters (see also Gal 2:10), shows there was a historical basis for the picture Luke describes. Acts also stresses the Temple piety of the Jerusalem Jewish Christians: "They went to the Temple together every day" (2:46; 3:1). Certainly such a context is that of Simeon to whom the Nunc Dimittis is attributed and also that of Zechariah, the priestly spokesman of the Benedictus.[20]

To be exact, however, such specificities (Poor Ones, at Jerusalem, with Temple piety) are shrewd speculations about the origins of the canticles, and they cannot be proved. Sometimes they are tied in with another, even more unprovable, thesis that the canticles were translated into Greek from Hebrew or Aramaic, presumably the language of the first Christians. For our purposes it is better to be content with the simple probability that the canticles are (from a collection of?) the hymns of an early Jewish Christian group[21] without being more specific. Thus the church's frequent and sometimes daily use of them in the liturgy recovers their origin in the sense that we are reciting the words that our most ancient ancestors in the faith used as community praise of God.

Has Luke done violence if, as we theorize, he has taken over these canticles and placed them on the lips of Infancy Narrative figures like Mary, Zechariah, and Simeon? To the contrary, his insight is most appropriate: If these were the

[20]Although Acts' description does not say that the Jerusalem Christians sang hymns, 2:47 speaks of their praising God, and technically the canticles of the Infancy Narrative are to be categorized as hymns of praise.

[21]"Early," not only because they are preLucan, but also because their christology is phrased entirely in Old Testament language, unlike the developed hymns we find in post-50 Christian writings.

The Benedictus

hymns of early Jewish Christians, they now appear in the Gospel on the lips of the first Jewish believers in the good news about John the Baptist and Jesus.[22] Going beyond this general connaturality, Luke has skillfully made his canticles match the spokespersons, often following leads in the narrative. In 1:40 we are told that Mary greeted Elizabeth, but no words are reported; the insertion of the Magnificat (1:46-55) supplies her with words that (as we shall see) are most appropriate. In the narrative (1:64) we read that Zechariah began to speak in praise of God, but again no words are recorded; the insertion of the Benedictus in 1:68-79 supplies that praise of God. That the spokespersons are different is also respected. The beginning of the Magnificat echoes the opening of Hannah's hymn in 1 Samuel 2:1-2 (Greek: "My heart is strengthened in the Lord; my horn is exalted in my God . . . I delight in Your salvation"). The appropriateness goes beyond the same gender of the speakers; Hannah's canticle is in the context of having given birth to her firstborn son, while Mary has just conceived her firstborn. As we shall see, although the Magnificat is a mosaic of Old Testament words and themes, some of the lines also anticipate Jesus' Beatitudes in Luke's account of the ministry. Such a reaching forward is appropriate on Mary's lips because she is a Gospel-ministry figure who has been brought back to Luke's "bridge" chapters of the Infancy Narrative. She encounters Old Testament figures like Zechariah and Simeon whose canticles do not have such clear anticipations of Gospel wording.

After these general remarks on the origin and the placing of the canticles in Luke 1-2, let me turn more specifically to the canticle that greets the conception and birth of John the Baptist and thus constitutes the sequence to the preceding essay in this book.

[22]As I pointed out, the appropriateness is enhanced if the Jewish Christian authors were "Poor Ones" with lives of Temple piety: Mary is a Poor One, and Zechariah and Simeon are exemplary of Temple piety.

The Benedictus

THE BENEDICTUS

(Luke 1:68-79)

Introductory Praise
    ⁶⁸ᵃ"Blessed be the Lord, the God of Israel:

First Strophe
    ⁶⁸ᵇBecause He has visited
    ⁶⁸ᶜand accomplished the redemption of His people,
    ⁶⁹ᵃand has raised up for us a horn of salvation
    ⁶⁹ᵇin the house of David His servant,
    ⁷⁰ as He spoke by the mouth of His holy prophets from of old:
    ⁷¹ᵃsalvation from our enemies
    ⁷¹ᵇand from the hand of all those who hate us,

Second Strophe
    ⁷²ᵃShowing mercy to our fathers
    ⁷²ᵇand remembering His holy covenant,
    ⁷³ the oath which He swore to our father Abraham,
    to grant us ⁷⁴that, without fear,
    delivered from the hands of our enemies,
    we might serve Him ⁷⁵in holiness and justice,
    before Him all the days of our lives.

Lucan Insertion
    ⁷⁶ᵃ*But you, child, will be called prophet of the Most High;*
    ⁷⁶ᵇ*for you will go before the Lord to make ready His ways,*
    ⁷⁷ᵃ*to grant to His people knowledge of salvation*
    ⁷⁷ᵇ*in the forgiveness of their sins.*

Conclusion
    ⁷⁸ᵃThrough the heartfelt mercy of our God
    ⁷⁸ᵇby which there has visited us a rising light from on high,
    ⁷⁹ᵃappearing to those who sat in darkness and the shadow of death,
    ⁷⁹ᵇguiding our feet into the way of peace."

The Benedictus

To accompany this discussion I have supplied a translation,[23] incorporating the analysis and division I deem most plausible. (Other scholars favor a slightly different division, but the differences would not really affect our discussion here.) In the classification of hymns that was developed for analyzing the Old Testament psalms, the Benedictus would most closely resemble a hymn of praise; and it does begin with the praise of the God of Israel. Clearly, the Jewish Christians who composed this canticle thought of themselves as continuing to belong to Israel. This same blessing of the God of Israel occurs at the end of three sections or "books" of the psalter, a work attributed to David (Pss 41:14 [13]; 72:18; 106:48), but also in 1 Kings 1:48 on the lips of David after Solomon's enthronization. That is appropriate, for the Jewish Christian authors of the canticle are praising what God has done in the last anointed king of David's lineage.

The original messianic reference of the canticle is retained even after Luke has placed it in the context of the Baptist's birth. Although Zechariah is praising God for his child, the lines that Luke has inserted in reference to that child (1:76-77: the Lucan adaptation of the canticle) will make clear that the salvific action for Israel comes not from the Baptist but from the Lord before whom the Baptist only prepares the way.[24] The subordination of the Baptist to the implicit main subject of the canticle, i.e., the messianic agent of God, is further indicated by where Luke places the inserted verses 76-77 pertinent to the Baptist. They do not stand at the end lest they appear to be the culmination of the praise; they stand before

[23]Taken from my *Birth of the Messiah* 366-67.

[24]Probably Luke's use of "the Lord" is deliberately ambiguous: in his own lifetime the Baptist thought he was preparing for the direct intervention of the Lord God of Israel, but the one who came after the Baptist was Jesus, child of Mary, whom Elizabeth lauded in 1:43 as "the mother of my Lord."

The Benedictus

a final poetic description (78-79) of the "rising light from on high"[25] who embodies "the heartfelt mercy of our God." Always the proper sequence must be kept: the Baptist did not constitute an end in himself, for as John 1:8 will insist: "He was not the light, but came to bear witness to the light." The Baptist is mentioned before Jesus, but Jesus is the one who guides out from darkness and death (Luke 1:79)—the work of the Messiah in the salvific action of God.

This salvific action, which supplies the motive for the praise of the God of Israel in the canticle, is described in the two strophes that constitute its body. These strophes are of approximately the same length and have similar structure. Each begins with what God has done by way of mercy and redemption for His people, "our fathers"; and each then proceeds to describe how this has been done for "us," filling promises respectively to David and to Abraham. We recall that the Matthean genealogy spoke of "Jesus Christ, Son of David, Son of Abraham." Matthew himself may have put together the elements of that genealogy, but he derived from Christian tradition the importance of those two ancestors who symbolized not only the special Jewish descent (David) of Jesus but also his wider reach (Paul uses Abraham to make the Gentiles sharers in the promises of God fulfilled in Jesus). Thus the Benedictus and the genealogy express in different ways an important common theme in the preparation for the coming of Jesus.

The first strophe indicates that the messianic inheritance from David was anticipated by the prophets (2 Samuel [chapter 7] was a prophetic book), while the second strophe connects Abraham with the covenant. The fulfillment of the Prophets and the Law is a motif that we have already seen in

[25]This is the Greek word *anatolē* which is used in Zechariah 3:8; 6:12 to translate the Hebrew references to the Davidic "branch" or "shoot." It is the same word used in Matthew 2:2 in the description of "His star at its *rising*," the star that signals the birth of the King of the Jews.

The Benedictus

the Lucan Infancy Narrative. Notice that the salvific action is described in the two strophes in past (aorist) tenses,[26] even though in the flow of the narrative Christ, the Lord, has not yet been born at Bethlehem. That is intelligible, for Jewish Christians composed the canticle after the resurrection when all this had already happened and the Messiah had come. In the Infancy Narrative context Zechariah is described as uttering a prophecy (1:67), and the past tenses show the surety of that prophetic view of what the Messiah would accomplish.

One may call the Benedictus a christological hymn since it concerns the Messiah, the "horn of salvation" (1:69; cf. Hannah's canticle in 1 Sam 2:10: "the horn of His anointed" [= Messiah, Christ]). Yet it is very different from the christological hymns we find in the Pauline and Johannine traditions, which spell out the human career of Jesus. For instance a hymn that Paul quotes in Philippians 2:6-11 speaks of Jesus' origins, his humble life as a servant, his obedient death on the cross, and his exaltation. The Johannine Prologue hymn (John 1:1-18) speaks of his coming into the world, being rejected by his own, and manifesting his glory. The Benedictus, however, describes the messianic salvation entirely in Old Testament terms without appealing to any event in Jesus' life. One cannot explain that phenomenon simply from the fact that in the narrative context in which Luke has placed the canticle none of the events of Jesus' life had yet taken place, for Luke did not hesitate to insert references to what the Baptist would do. Rather, in the Benedictus and in the other Lucan canticles (for the same phenomenon is true of them), we are hearing very early Christian christology that did not require and perhaps had not yet acquired a peculiarly

[26]The manuscripts do not agree whether to read an aorist or a future form in the key verb of the conclusion, thus "visited" or "will visit" in 1:78. I prefer the aorist, thinking that the scribes have conformed this description of Jesus to the future tenses that precede in the inserted description of the Baptist (1:76-77).

The Benedictus

Christian vocabulary—*perhaps the oldest preserved Christian prayers of praise* wherein Jewish believers expressed themselves entirely in the language of their ancestors. I have sometimes asked Jews of today who believe in the coming of a personal messiah whether, if someone whom they considered as worthy of that title were to come, they could recite the Benedictus (without the inserted Lucan verses 76-77). None of them found it alien language. Such an insight shows how appropriate is the use of the Benedictus as an Advent Gospel reading. This is the season where we relive the story of Israel and its expectations; we who believe that that story is encapsulated in Jesus and those expectations are fulfilled in him praise God in the language of Israel when we recite the Benedictus.

The Benedictus

Chapter 6

The Annunciation to Mary, the Visitation, and the Magnificat (Luke 1:26-56)

Of all the scenes that the church uses in the Advent liturgy, these Lucan episodes would be best known to Christians. And certainly this is the annunciation par excellence, far more famous than the annunciations to Joseph and to Zechariah. This is the annunciation that has been taken up so frequently in theology, spirituality, art, and literature. Seeking necessarily to be selective amidst the wealth of material offered by these scenes, I have chosen as best fitting the Advent motif of this book the Lucan presentation of Mary as a model disciple in receiving and reacting to the Gospel message. In this emphasis, however, a caution is necessary. Some scholars, mostly Catholic, have wished to rename this scene the calling of Mary as if its primary message was about her. I reject that firmly: The primary message is centered on the conception of Jesus as Messiah and God's Son and what he will accomplish by way of salvation for those who depend on God. Nevertheless, exhibiting true Christian instinct that the gospel is not good *news* unless there is someone to hear it, Luke presents Mary as the first to hear and accept it and then to proclaim it. Thus he holds her up as the first and model disciple.[27] The vocation of the disciple is not the primary message of the scene, but a necessary corollary and one that well serves our Advent motif.

In discussing Mary's discipleship we should be aware that we know very little about the psychology and personal feel-

[27]It is worth noting that this is not a peculiarly Catholic view. It was clearly advocated by the Finnish Lutheran scholar, H. Räisänen; and it has been accepted from him by the ecumenical study *Mary in the New Testament*, ed. R. E. Brown, *et al.* (New York: Paulist, 1978).

Annunciation to Mary, the Visitation, and the Magnificat

ings of the historical Mary;[28] yet here Luke gives us our strongest New Testament evidence for the massively important fact that she was a disciple of Jesus. How important that is can be appreciated when we realize that one could not derive it from Mark. That Gospel clearly distinguishes between Mary (accompanied by Jesus' brothers or male relatives) on the one hand and his disciples on the other hand, with only the latter placed in the context of doing the will of God (Mark 3:31-35). Mark has a deprecatory attitude toward Jesus' family who think he is beside himself and do not honor him (3:21; 6:4). Even Matthew, who knows that Mary conceived Jesus through the Holy Spirit and so excises the deprecatory statements of Mark about the family, never clarifies that Mary became a disciple. Only John exhibits the same positive view as Luke on this question of specifically bringing Jesus' mother into the family of disciples; for he describes Jesus as constituting her to be the mother of the disciple whom he loves (the model disciple) and thus gives her a shared preeminence in discipleship. Reflecting on the role of Mary as a preeminent disciple was probably a second-stage development in New Testament thought. After Christians had reflected on the mystery of Jesus, they turned to reflect on how he impinged on those who were close to him physically and then included that reflection in the "good news."[29]

THE ANNUNCIATION

Following the same format he used to introduce the annunciation to Zechariah, Luke introduces this scene with notes on time, place, and the primary characters. The time (the sixth month, i.e., of Elizabeth's pregnancy) helps to call the reader's attention to the relationship between the two annunciations. For the previous annunciation, the place was Jerusalem

[28]See above in chapter 1 for some general remarks on historical problems.
[29]Written earlier than Luke or John, Mark is very christologically focused and does not include in its scope this wider understanding of the gospel.

Annunciation to Mary, the Visitation, and the Magnificat

and the heritage was priestly—circumstances befitting Old Testament characters like Zechariah and Elizabeth. In this annunciation the place is Nazareth in Galilee and the heritage is Davidic—circumstances befitting Gospel characters like Mary and Joseph intimately involved with Jesus, whose public ministry will be in Galilee and who is the Messiah of the house of David.[30]

A close comparison of the introductions to the two Lucan annunciations reveals an even more significant difference between them. Zechariah and Elizabeth in their piety have been yearning for a child, so that the conception of the Baptist was in part God's answer to Zechariah's prayers (Luke 1:13); but Mary is a virgin who has not yet been intimate with her husband, so that what happens is not a response to her yearning but a surprise initiative by God that neither Mary nor Joseph could have anticipated. The Baptist's conception, while a gift of God, involved an act of human intercourse. Mary's conception involves a divine creative action without human intercourse; it is the work of the overshadowing Spirit, that same Spirit that hovered at the creation of the world when all was void (Gen 1:2; see p. 36 above). When one compares the Gabriel-Zechariah and Gabriel-Mary dialogues, there is a similarity of format, flowing from the set pattern of annunciations of birth that one can find in the Old Testament accounts of the births of Ishmael, Isaac, and Samson,[31] and that also appears in Matthew's annunciation of

[30]Interestingly, despite their very different annunciations of Jesus' birth, Matthew and Luke agree on the status and situation of the parents: Joseph is of the house of David; Mary is a virgin; yet they are married—both use the less customary verb *mnēsteuein* to describe this marriage where the principals do not yet live together (footnote 7 above). Luke pays less attention than Matthew, however, to how Jesus would have David lineage when Joseph did not beget him; see pp. 33-34 above.

[31]Genesis 16:7-12; chapters 17–18; Judges 13:3-20. In the pattern the appearance of (an angel of) the Lord leads the visionary to fear or prostration. Then the heavenly messenger addresses the visionary, usually by name, some-

Annunciation to Mary, the Visitation, and the Magnificat

Jesus' birth. Nevertheless, despite similarities, throughout Luke underlines the uniqueness of Jesus who, even in conception and birth, is greater than the Baptist (Luke 3:16).

Worthy of note is Gabriel's addressing Mary in 1:28 as "Favored One." This has the connotation of being especially graced, whence the Latin translation that gave rise to the "full of grace." The favor or grace that Mary "has found with God" (1:30) is explained in 1:31 in future terms: She will conceive and give birth to Jesus. The address "Favored One" anticipates that future favor with certitude, but it also corresponds to a status that Mary has already enjoyed. The one whom God has chosen for the conception of His Son is one who has already enjoyed His grace by the way she has lived. Her discipleship, as we shall see, comes into being when she says yes to God's will about Jesus; but such readiness is possible for her because by God's grace she has said yes to Him before. Thus Mary's discipleship does not exhibit conversion but consistency. The same may be true for many of us at those unique moments when we are conscious of being invited to say yes to God's will in something important.

The heart of the annunciation to Mary concerns the twofold identity of Jesus, the child to be conceived—an identity that was also central in Matthew's annunciation to Joseph. The identity of the Messiah as the Son of David goes back in Jewish thought to 2 Samuel 7 where Nathan promises David that he will have an enduring line of descendants who will rule over Israel forever. Luke makes this explicit in 1:32-33 by hav-

---

times with an added phrase pertinent to the visionary's role, and urges, "Do not fear." The message is that the future mother is or will be with child to whom she will give birth—a child who is to be named X (sometimes with an explanatory etymology) and whose accomplishments will be Y. The visionary poses an objection as to how this can be, sometimes asking for a sign. Some of these features, plus others pertinent to Luke's annunciation, are found in angelic annunciations of vocation, e.g., of Moses in Exodus 3:2-12; of Gideon in Judges 6:12-23.

Annunciation to Mary, the Visitation, and the Magnificat

ing Gabriel quote that promise from 2 Samuel in a slightly rephrased manner (evidently customary at this time as we can see in the Dead Sea Scrolls). The following comparison of the wording shows this:

Luke 1:

32a "He will be great and will be called Son of the Most High.
32b And the Lord God will give him the throne of his father David;
33a and he will be king over the house of Jacob forever,
33b and there will be no end to his kingdom."

2 Sam 7:

9 "I shall make for you a *great* name . . .
13 I shall establish *the throne of his kingdom forever.*
14 I shall be his father, and he will be *my son* . . .
16 And your *house* and your *kingdom* will be made sure *forever.*"

Mary's questioning response (stereotypic of such annunciations), "How can this be?", and her insistence that she has not had relations with a man allow Gabriel to explain God's role and thus highlight the other half of Jesus' identity. He is not only Son of David, he is Son of God (1:35):

"The Holy Spirit will come upon you
and power from the Most High will overshadow you.
Therefore, the child to be born will be called holy—Son of God."

This is not the language of Old Testament prophecy but of New Testament preaching. In the introductory chapter to this book I noted how set elements of a description of Jesus as Son of God were reused in various parts of the New Testament in reference to different aspects of Jesus' career (his parousia, resurrection, baptism, and now his conception) as part of the essential task of proclaiming who he was. The Pauline phraseology in Romans 1:3-4, which Paul knew from earlier preaching, is particularly close to Luke's presentation of Jesus' twofold identity in the annunciation:

"Born of the seed of David according to the flesh;
designated Son of God in power according to the Holy Spirit."

Annunciation to Mary, the Visitation, and the Magnificat

Thus, in revealing to Mary the identity of Jesus, Gabriel is speaking both the language of the Old Testament prophets about the Son of David and the language of the New Testament preachers about the Son of God—language that Paul in Romans specifically calls "gospel." Thus it is no exaggeration to say that for Luke Mary has heard the gospel of Jesus Christ, and indeed is the first one to have done so.

In all of this Luke has anticipated a christological terminology that is appropriate to Jesus' ministry and beyond. He continues that anticipation in describing Mary's basic response to the gospel she has heard. In the common tradition of Jesus' ministry shared by the first three Gospels, Mary appears in only one scene (Mark 3:31-35; Matthew 12:46-50; Luke 8:19-21). That scene interprets the relationship of Jesus' natural family to his disciples by having Jesus define family, not in terms of physical descent, but in terms of accepting his gospel about God: "Whoever does the will of God is my brother, and sister, and mother" (Mark 3:35) or, more pertinently, in the Lucan form, "My mother and my brothers are those who hear the word of God and do it" (Luke 8:21). When in the annunciation Luke reports Mary's answer, "Let it be done to me according to your word," he is describing not only one who is consenting to be the physical mother of Jesus but also and very importantly one who meets Jesus' criterion for his family of disciples—indeed the first one.

Read in Advent, Luke's message in this annunciation is as pertinent as when he first wrote it. We Christians must be very clear as to what we believe about the identity of the one to be born at Christmas. He is not just the Prince of Peace, the title that even noncommittal media commentators are willing to give him. He is the Messiah of the house of David, embodying in himself all that rich Old Testament background that these Advent passages have evoked again and again. Beyond that he is the unique Son of God, the very presence of God with us. Anything less is not the gospel, and assent to

Annunciation to Mary, the Visitation, and the Magnificat

anything less will not make us disciples. And assent to that double identity is not just an intellectual assent; it involves being willing to hear Jesus' proclamation of God's will and doing it.

THE VISITATION AND THE MAGNIFICAT

As part of the annunciation, Gabriel tells Mary (1:36-37), "Your relative Elizabeth, despite her old age, has also conceived a son; indeed, this is the sixth month for a woman who was deemed barren. Nothing said by God can be impossible."[32] That verse prepares for the visitation of Mary to Elizabeth, which brings together the mothers affected by the two annunciations. Accordingly, when Luke tells us (1:39) that, after the angel departed, Mary arose and went hastily into the hill country of Judea to the house of Zechariah, he is not describing simply her eagerness to see her relative. Precisely because the angel spoke of Elizabeth's pregnancy as part of the plan of God, Mary's haste reflects her obedience to that plan.

Elizabeth's prophetic greeting is of interest in Luke's portrait of Mary's discipleship. During the public ministry a woman in the crowd will shout out a blessing (macarism) in praise of Jesus: "Fortunate is the womb that bore you and the breasts you sucked" (11:27—a scene peculiar to Luke). This is a very Jewish blessing echoing the sentiment of Deuteronomy 28:1, 4 where a benediction was promised to Israel if it would be obedient to the voice of God: "Blessed be the fruit of your womb." In saying to Mary, "Blessed are you among women[33] and blessed is the fruit of your womb," Elizabeth, like the woman in the crowd, is appreciating not only the joy of Mary's being the mother of a son, but the

[32]This last sentence is still another echo of the Abraham-Sarah story which is so prominent in Luke's portrait of Zechariah-Elizabeth (Gen 18:14).

[33]This line of the blessing echoes a praise of distinguished women of Israel: Jael (Judg 5:24) and Judith (Jud 13:18).

Annunciation to Mary, the Visitation, and the Magnificat

enormous honor of being the physical mother of the Messiah. In the ministry, however, Jesus reacted to that praise with the same instinct that he showed in the scene concerning the relationship of discipleship to natural family (discussed above). He corrected the woman in the crowd, "Fortunate rather are those who hear the word of God and keep it" (Luke 11:28). Elizabeth is the mother of a prophet; and being filled with the Holy Spirit (1:41), she can supply her own modification. After blessing Mary's physical motherhood, she goes on to say climactically, "Fortunate is she who believed that the Lord's word to her would be fulfilled." This reiterates the supreme importance of hearing the word of God and doing it, and anticipates Jesus' own encomium of his mother (Luke 8:21). Mary is doubly blessed; she is the physical mother of the Messiah and one who meets the criterion for Jesus' family of disciples. The fact that the mother of the Baptist utters this blessing with the babe literally jumping with joy in her womb (1:44) is an anticipation of the Baptist's own witness to the one to come after him.

Thus far in the interchange between the two women during the visitation, Elizabeth has twice blessed Mary. Noblesse oblige would almost require that Mary in turn bless Elizabeth. But in Luke's vision of the scene this is the appropriate moment to insert the Magnificat with the clear effect that if Elizabeth blesses Mary, "the mother of my Lord" (1:43), Mary now blesses the Lord himself. The preceding chapter discussed how the Lucan infancy canticles exhibit the style of the Jewish psalmody of this era in being mosaics of Old Testament passages. That is true of the Magnificat in particular.

On p. 54 above, we noted that the opening of the Magnificat is a deliberate parallel to the opening of Hannah's canticle after the birth of her child in 1 Samuel 2:1-2. The Hannah parallelism continues throughout the Magnificat, e.g., Luke 1:48, "Because He has regarded the low estate of

Annunciation to Mary, the Visitation, and the Magnificat

His handmaid," echoes the prayer in 1 Samuel 1:11, "O Lord
of Hosts, if you will look on the low estate of your handmaid." This handmaid motif was anticipated by Luke in 1:38
where "Behold the handmaid of the Lord" was part of
Mary's final response to Gabriel. The term employed is literally the feminine form of "slave"; and besides the religious
context of servants of the Lord (see Acts 2:18), it may reflect
the sociological situation of many early Christians. When the
Roman governor Pliny in the early second century went looking for Christians to find out what this strange group was,
he turned to slavewomen because among such lowly crea-
tures he was likely to find Christians. That Mary designates
herself a handmaid is poetically beautiful in our hearing, but
to outsiders in early times it would be another confirmation
that Christianity was bizarre: a group consisting of many
slaves, worshiping a crucified criminal. Whether or not the
Magnificat came from an early Christian group of "Poor
Ones" (see preceding chapter), it clearly shares their mentality. Mary has become the spokeswoman of their ideals.

That same mentality dominates the body of the Magnificat
describing the salvific action of God (1:51-53):

"He has shown His strength with His arm;
He has scattered the proud in the imagination of their hearts.
He has put down the mighty from their thrones
and has exalted those of low degree.
He has filled the hungry with good things,
and the rich He has sent away empty."

This section continues the parallelism with Hannah's hymn
(1 Sam 2:7-8):

"The Lord makes poor and makes rich;
He reduces to lowliness and He lifts up.
He lifts the needy from the earth;
and from the dung heap He raises up the poor
to seat them with the mighty,
making them inherit a throne of glory."

Annunciation to Mary, the Visitation, and the Magnificat

Yet in the conciseness of its antitheses the Magnificat does more than echo Hannah and the Old Testament; it anticipates the gospel message, especially the Beatitudes and Woes spoken by Jesus in Luke 6:20-26. I know that most readers are familiar with Matthew's eight Beatitudes and the hallowed phrasing of "poor in spirit" and "hunger and thirst after justice." But Luke has only four Beatitudes, and like sharp hammer blows they have no mollifying, spiritualizing clauses like "in spirit" or "after justice":

"Blessed are you who are poor, for yours is the kingdom of God.
Blessed are you who are hungry now, for you shall be satisfied.
Blessed are you who weep now, for you shall laugh.
Blessed are you when all hate you . . ., your reward is great in
heaven."

And so that the reader will not miss that Jesus is talking about concrete poor, hungry, and suffering people, Luke follows this with four antithetical Woes uttered by Jesus:

"Woe to you who are rich, for you have received your consolation.
Woe to you who are full now, for you shall hunger.
Woe to you who laugh now, for you shall mourn and weep.
Woe to you when all speak well of you, for so their fathers did
to the false prophets."

The Magnificat, historically composed after Jesus had proclaimed such a gospel, reuses Jesus' antithetical style to celebrate what God has done, exalting the low and the hungry, putting down the proud, the mighty, and the rich.

By placing this canticle on Mary's lips, however, Luke has made a statement about discipleship and gospel. We have seen that in the annunciation Mary becomes the first disciple, indeed, the first Christian, by hearing the word, i.e., the good news of Jesus' identity as Messiah and God's Son, and by accepting it. In the visitation she hastens to share this gospel word with others, and now in the Magnificat we have her interpretation of that word, resembling the interpretation that her son had given it in the ministry. This sequence gives

Annunciation to Mary, the Visitation, and the Magnificat

us an important insight on christology and its interpretation. At the beginning of the public ministry in Luke's Gospel (as in the other Gospels) God's voice identifies Jesus as His Beloved Son (3:22)—the good news from the start is christological. But when Jesus speaks the gospel to people, he does not reiterate his own identity to people saying, "I am God's Son." Rather he interprets what the sending of the Son means, so that the Beatitudes and the Woes show both its salvific and judgmental results. In the Infancy Narrative Mary has heard from Gabriel the christological identity of Jesus; but when she gives voice interpreting what she has heard, she does not proclaim the greatness of the saving God because He has sent the Messiah, His Son. Rather, her praise of Him interprets the sending: He has shown strength, exalting the lowly, filling the hungry. In short (Luke 1:54-55):

"He has helped His servant Israel
in remembrance of His mercy,
as He spoke unto our fathers,
to Abraham and his posterity forever."

The first Christian disciple exemplifies the essential task of discipleship. After hearing the word of God and accepting it, we must share it with others, not by simply repeating it but by interpreting so that they can see it truly as *good* news. As we look forward in Advent to the coming of Christ, let us ask ourselves how this year we are going to interpret for others what we believe happens at Christmas, so that they will be able to appreciate what the angel announced at the first Christmas (Luke 2:10-11). "I announce to you good news of a great joy which will be for the whole people: To you this day there is born in the city of David a savior who is Messiah and Lord."

***

Annunciation to Mary, the Visitation, and the Magnificat

Let me close this chapter in this book with the remarks of perhaps the most theologically perceptive and nuanced deceased pope of this century, Paul VI, as contained in the last significant document he wrote on Mary (*Marialis Cultus*, February 1974). I cannot phrase better what the Bible tells us about Mary in the Infancy Narratives and elsewhere:

> "The Virgin Mary has always been proposed to the faithful by the church as an example to be imitated, not precisely in the type of life she led and much less for the sociocultural background in which she lived and which scarcely today exists anywhere. Rather she is held up as an example to the faithful for the way in which in her own particular life she fully and responsibly accepted the will of God, because she heard the word of God and acted on it, and because charity and the spirit of service were the driving force of her actions. She is worthy of imitation because she was the first and most perfect of Christ's disciples."

Annunciation to Mary, the Visitation, and the Magnificat

Works of Raymond E. Brown published by The Liturgical Press:

A Coming Christ in Advent (Matthew 1 and Luke 1)
An Adult Christ at Christmas (Matthew 2 and Luke 2)
A Crucified Christ in Holy Week (Passion Narratives)
A Risen Christ in Eastertime (Resurrection Narratives)
A Once-and-Coming Spirit at Pentecost (Acts and John)

The Gospels and Epistles of John—A Concise Commentary
The New Jerome Bible Handbook, edited with J. A. Fitzmyer and
  R. E. Murphy